Women Writers

Doris Lessing

Margaret Moan Rowe

MACMILLAN

First published 1994 by
THE MACMILLAN PRESS LTD
Houndmills, Basingstoke, Hampshire RG21 2XS
and London
Companies and representatives
throughout the world

ISBN 0–333–55486–8 hardcover
ISBN 0–333–55487–6 paperback

A catalogue record for this book is available from the British Library.

Copy-edited and typeset by Povey–Edmondson
Okehampton and Rochdale, England

Printed in China

Contents

To Jessie Moan
From her impertinent and loving daughter

Acknowledgements

My hope is that both new and veteran readers of Doris Lessing's fiction will find my readings illuminating. Yet no work, however illuminating or unique, is without its debt to others. No one writing on Doris Lessing can ignore the impressive body of existing criticism. My own debt to others with published views is specified in my text.

Here I wish to pay different debts. My thanks to graduate students at Purdue University who worked with me in two seminars on Lessing's fiction. Thanks also to colleagues for suggestions and support: Thomas Adler, Ann Astell, Marianne Boruch, William Stuckey of Purdue University, and last, but never least, Alan Wilde of Temple University.

A complete manuscript, however, does not publish itself. I am grateful to Margaret Cannon, Gloria Hart and Cathryn Tanner at the publishers, and to Keith Povey and Elizabeth Black who did the editing. Doris Lessing generously agreed to my extensive use of her work, and I thank her.

Finally, I want to express affectionate gratitude to my husband Willam Rowe for his constant encouragement.

West Lafayette, Indiana   MARGARET MOAN ROWE

The author and publishers wish to thank the following for permission to use copyright material:

HarperCollins Publishers for material from Doris Lessing, *Martha Quest*, 1970, and *The Grass Is Singing*, 1976; and with Alfred A. Knopf, Inc. for Doris Lessing, *The Four-Gated City*. Copyright © 1969 by Doris Lessing.

The Octagon Press Ltd for material from Doris Lessing, *The Memoirs of a Survivor*, 1976.

Penguin Books Ltd for material from Doris Lessing, *The Grass Is Singing*, Michael Joseph, 1950. Copyright © Doris Lessing, 1950; and Doris Lessing, *The Golden Notebook*, Michael Joseph, 1962. Copyright © Doris Lessing, 1962.

Random Century Group with Alfred A. Knopf, Inc. for material from Doris Lessing, *The Making of the Representative for Planet 8*, Jonathan Cape, 1988. Copyright © 1982 by Doris Lessing; and Doris Lessing, *The Fifth Child*, Jonathan Cape, 1988. Copyright © 1988 by Doris Lessing.

Editors' Preface

The study of women's writing has been long neglected by a male critical establishment both in academic circles and beyond. As a result, many women writers have either been unfairly neglected or have been marginalised in some way, so that their true influence and importance has been ignored. Other women writers have been accepted by male critics and academics, but on terms which seem, to many women readers of this generation, to be false or simplistic. In the past the internal conflicts involved in being a women in a male-dominated society have been largely ignored by readers of both sexes, and this has affected our reading of women's work. The time has come for a serious reassessment of women's writings in the light of what we understand today.

This series is designed to help in that reassessment.

All the books are written by women because we believe that men's understanding of feminist critique is only, at best, partial. And besides, men have held the floor quite long enough.

EVA FIGES
ADELE KING

A Note on Editions

Quotations from Doris Lessing's work are taken from the paperback editions listed below. Dates in brackets are original publication dates. In my text, I note abbreviated book titles and page numbers in parentheses after quotations.

Fiction

GS	*The Grass Is Singing*	Plume Books	1976	[1950]
HL	*The Habit of Loving*	Plume Books	1976	[1957]

CHILDREN OF VIOLENCE

MQ	*Martha Quest*	Plume Books	1970	[1952]
PM	*A Proper Marriage*	Plume Books	1970	[1954]
RS	*A Ripple from the Storm*	Plume Books	1970	[1958]
L	*Landlocked*	Plume Books	1970	[1965]
F-G	*The Four-Gated City*	Plume Books	1976	[1969]

GN	*The Golden Notebook*	Bantam Books	1973	[1962]
B	*Briefing for a Descent into Hell*	Vintage Books	1981	[1971]
SD	*The Summer Before the Dark*	Bantam Books	1974	[1973]
M	*The Memoirs of a Survivor*	Bantam Books	1976	[1974]

CANOPUS IN ARGOS: ARCHIVES

S	*Shikasta*	Vintage Books	1981	[1979]
MBZ	*Marriages Between Zones Three, Four, and Five*	Vintage Books	1981	[1980]
SE	*The Sirian Experiments*	Vintage Books	1982	[1981]
P8	*The Making of the Representative for Planet 8*	Vintage Books	1988	[1982]

SA	*The Sentimental Agents*	Vintage Books	1984	[1983]
DJS	*The Diaries of Jane Somers: The Diary of a Good Neighbour and If the Old Could. . .*	Vintage Books	1984	[1983]
GT	*The Good Terrorist*	Vintage Books	1986	[1985]
FC	*The Fifth Child*	Vintage Books	1988	[1988]

Collections of Essays

SPV	*A Small Personal Voice,* ed. Paul Schlueter	Vintage Books	1975	[1975]
P	*Prisons We Choose to Live Inside*	Perennial Library	1987	[1987]

1 The Far Counties: Lessing's Early Years

the BBC, the *Observer* and Stephen King-Hall's news-
letters about British politics were more real to her
parents than anything which happened in, or came out
of, Rhodesia.

C. J. Driver[1]

Doris Lessing was born in Kermanshah, Persia, on 22
October 1919. She began life as Doris May Taylor, the first
child of Emily Maude McVeagh and Alfred Cook Taylor
who had left (escaped) England after the Great War to
pursue a freer, less constrained life in the East. By the time
Doris Taylor was 5, Alfred Taylor, once again, felt too
constricted by protocols – this time associated with the life
of a British banker in Persia – and decided 'to light out for
the territory', the Southern Rhodesia that would later
become Zimbabwe.

But Alfred Taylor was no Huckleberry Finn. Seduced by
the promises of an Empire Exhibition, Taylor responded
to a colonial government that offered cheap land; he
invested all his capital, securing a large tract of land,
3000 acres, and a very small house in Africa. The Southern Rhodesia that the Taylors entered in 1927 was largely
the creation of white colonists, like the Taylors, arriving
and claiming already-occupied land. Nobody asked the
black native population about the promises of the Empire
Exhibition; the Africans were just moved to make way for
progress. Years later Lessing reviewed Lawrence Vambe's

An Ill-fated People: Zimbabwe Before and After Rhodes
and described the 'white development' of Rhodesia:

> The Africans were put into native reserves. The Native
> Reserves of Rhodesia, like those of South Africa, had,
> and have, the poorest soil, the least water, the worst of
> everything, from roads to shops. It is almost impossible
> to convey to people in Britain what a Native Reserve is
> like. The nearest to it is perhaps Dartmoor, imagined
> hot and arid. On it are scattered groups of mud and
> grass huts, and a store, which is a brick room selling
> cloth goods and the cheapest of groceries. There are no
> good roads, telephones, cinemas, facilities for sport or
> recreation. Into these deserts, completely cut off from
> modern life, are forcibly herded people whose way of life
> before the white man came was as wide, variegated, full
> of potential, as Africa itself. The white people began to
> steal the land as soon as they arrived in the country.
> They now have taken more than half of it, are always
> taking more and more and more.[2]

But the Taylors, like other white settlers, did not see
themselves as takers; they were landowners, British, and
white. They had a mandate to civilise.

Most of the colonists, fortunately or unfortunately, were
not adventurers on the scale of Cecil Rhodes. They fitted,
as Lessing notes, 'Olive Schreiner's definition of the South
Africans of her time as "a nation of petty bourgeois
philistines".'[3] The British society that dominated the
colony had turned it into the Far Counties and attempted
to mirror the experiences of home. In 'Flavours of Exile', a
short story published in *The Habit of Loving* (1957),
Lessing captures that obsession with replicating the experiences of home in the mother's attempt to transform
Africa into England – at least as far as vegetables were
concerned:

Year after year my mother yearned for Brussels sprouts, whose name came to represent to me something exotic and unattainable. When at last she managed to grow a dozen spikes of this plant in one cold winter that offered us sufficient frost, she of course sent a note to the MacGregors, so that they might share the treat. They came from Glasgow, they came from Home, and they could share the language of nostalgia. At the table, the four grownups ate the bitter little cabbages and agreed that the soil of Africa was unable to grow food that had any taste at all. I said scornfully that I couldn't see what all the fuss was about.

(HL, pp. 139–40)

Hierarchies in Southern Rhodesia, however, were not restricted to 'the vegetable kingdom'. Settlers imported class differences from home and intensified those class differences by wedding them to violent racial prejudices.

The Africans on the Native Reserves – the real exiles in the narrative of colonisation – were virtually invisible to the settlers, a fact of colonial life that would form the dramatic basis of Lessing's first novel *The Grass is Singing* (1950). Other non-Christian, non-white, or non-Northern European populations – Jews, Indians, and Greeks in particular – were tolerated as necessary evils, generally shopkeepers. The myth of community existed only for white faces and there only tenuously as Lessing describes in an early scene in *Martha Quest* (1952):

On mail days there were cars of every degree of wealth, from the enormous American cars of the tobacco farmers down to eccentric creations like the Quests', but the owners of the cars met together without any consciousness of degree, English and Scotch, Welsh and Irish, rich and poor, it was all backslapping and Christian names, a happy family atmosphere which had a touch of hyster-

ical necessity in it, since the mail days, gymkhanas and
dances were false tokens of community – for what is
community if not people who share their experience?

(MQ, pp. 44–5)

For Lessing's father the absence of rigid community and
social constraints was the promise of Eden, for her mother
the absence of community was hell.

Alfred Taylor saw the move as a way to realise his
dream of independence and the open life, but he had not
counted on the whims of nature or his own peculiar
detachment in his vision of the free life. For Maude
Taylor, described by her daughter as 'essentially urban',[4]
the move was nothing less than disaster, cutting her off
from the social life she had come to enjoy in Teheran. In an
early autobiographical essay, 'My Father', Lessing positioned her mother's urban preoccupations against her
father's daring. Alfred Taylor, according to his daughter,
acted 'on an impulse, turning his back forever on England,
washing his hands of the corruption of the East' and
'collected all his capital' for a new life in Rhodesia. For
the trek to Rhodesia, according to her daughter, Maude
Taylor 'packed curtains from Liberty's, clothes from
Harrods, visiting cards, a piano, Persian rugs, a governess
and two small children' (SPV, p. 90). Maude Taylor
packed up an English household; Alfred Taylor provided
the vision.

This psychological division between the visionary and
the ordinary, between two very different ways of seeing the
world that Lessing continually ascribes to her parents in
reminiscences, if destructive to actual family life, becomes
a productive tension in much of her fiction. Indeed from
Lessing's preoccupation with parent–child relationships in
The Grass Is Singing through to *The Fifth Child* (1988), one
can fairly surmise that the Taylors' differences and dis-
appointments played themselves out in the creative life of

their daughter who has noted: 'We use our parents like recurring dreams, to be entered into when needed; they are always there for love or for hate' (SPV, p. 83). She might also have added 'for inspiration'.

What is of particular interest about the recurring dream of parents that Lessing so often enters is the significance of the father. Let me begin my explanation by quoting Lessing again but this time from her sympathetic 'Afterword to *The Story of an African Farm* by Olive Schreiner' published in 1968. In that essay Lessing speculates about the shaping of a writer:

> To the creation of a woman novelist seem to go certain psychological ingredients; at least, often enough to make it interesting. One of them, a balance between father and mother where the practicality, the ordinary sense, cleverness, and worldly ambition is on the side of the mother; and the father's life is so weighted with dreams and ideas and imaginings that their joint life gets lost in what looks like a hopeless muddle and failure, but which holds a potentiality for something that must be recognised as better, on a different level, than what ordinary sense or cleverness can begin to conceive.
>
> (SPV, p. 108)

While the word 'balance' suggests some sort of equilibrium between the parents' qualities, the very qualities cited, especially 'ordinary sense' for the mother and the 'dreams and ideas and imaginings' that weight the father, favour the father. Indeed the very end of the observation argues for the triumph of imagination – how else to get to 'a different level' – over practicality – the limitations of 'ordinary sense or cleverness'.

I do not want to overestimate Lessing's regard for her father nor my own capacity for psychoanalysis, but awareness of the pull between the paternal and the

maternal is central to understanding Lessing's biography
and to much of the autobiographical slant of her fiction.
For a writer as biography-shy as she, Lessing has often
commented on the autobiographical element in the novel
as for instance in her 'Afterword' to Schreiner's novel
where she describes the novel form as 'that hybrid, the
mixture of journalism and the *Zeitgeist* and autobiography
that comes out of a part of the human consciousness which
is always trying to understand itself, to come into the light'
(SPV, p. 99).

In reminiscences, short stories, and most dramatically in
the *Children of Violence* series, Lessing presents the father
as dreamer, the mother as regulator; the father associated
with countryside and the natural world, the mother bound
to city values and social expectations; the father able to
detach himself from the mundane to gaze at the stars, the
mother clutching domestic objects; the father talking about
the universe, the mother complaining about school grades.
Lessing's fiction resonates with this parental division; let
me cite but one example. Toward the end of *A Proper
Marriage* (1954), Lessing presents Martha Quest's parents'
responses to the collapse of her marriage. Neither parent
actually supports the daughter, but Mr Quest moves
farther away from conventional responses when he speaks
words that cause Martha to realise her desire to escape her
marriage. Mrs Quest stands as the gatekeeper of convention when she refuses to harbour Martha after a violent
domestic quarrel: ' "Go back to him", she was saying, "it
serves you right". The door shut in Martha's face' (PM,
p. 603). In her reading of *Children of Violence*, Nicole
Ward Jouve asks 'isn't the father's eccentricity so much
more heartwarming than the mother's?'[5] The answer, I
think, is yes.

Jouve goes on to note that in *Children of Violence*: 'The
mother is never chosen: she is avoided, rebelled against,
fled from, even when she is actually closest.'[6] The same

thing happens when Doris Lessing lays claim to literary ancestry, when she shapes a story of cultural origins. At some point all well-known writers are asked to identify their influences, to name the writers who affected their youthful imaginations. Not unexpectedly Lessing has been asked or has volunteered such information; not unexpectedly, given her ethical concerns, she names nineteenth-century novelists. Tolstoy, she maintains in *Going Home* (1957), best explains the Africa in which she grew up: 'When I am asked to recommend novels which will describe white-settler Africa most accurately to those who don't know it, I always suggest a re-reading of those parts of *Anna Karenina* about the landowners and the peasants' (p. 19). Indeed, Tolstoy and other nineteenth-century male European writers form Doris Lessing's pantheon. As she notes in 'The Small Personal Voice': 'For me the highest point of literature was the novel of the nineteenth century, the work of Tolstoy, Stendhal, Dostoevsky, Balzac, Turgenev, Chekhov; the works of the great realists' (SPV, p. 4).

What is curious is the absence of nineteenth-century British novelists – male or female – in Lessing's testimony. Indeed, fourteen years after *Going Home* and 'The Small Personal Voice', she offered her most dismissive comment on the Victorian novel in her 1971 'Preface' to *The Golden Notebook*:

But a very useful Victorian novel never got itself written. Hardy tells us what it was like to be poor, to have an imagination larger than the possibilities of a very narrow time. George Eliot is good as far as she goes. But I think the penalty she paid for being a Victorian woman was that she had to be shown to be a good woman even when she wasn't according to the hypocrisies of the time – there is a great deal she does not understand because she is moral. Meredith, that astonishingly underrated,

writer is perhaps nearest. Trollope tried the subject
[describing the intellectual and moral climate of the
century] but lacked the scope. There isn't one novel
that has the vigour and conflict of ideas in action that is
in a good biography of William Morris.

(GN, xi)

Lessing obviously has a very conflicted relationship with
Victorianism. In words like 'narrow', 'victim', 'penalty',
and 'hypocrisies', Lessing is as much dismissing the
Victorian period – the age which produced her parents
and their inhibitions – as she is dismissing the literature.
But let me turn back to the literature and writers that
Lessing praises.

Lessing wanted to claim a European literary ancestry
especially in 'The Small Personal Voice', which appeared
in 1957, as a slap at the unwelcoming English who treated
her as a colonial after her emigration to England in 1949.
Claire Sprague notes that Lessing's list of favoured writers
is 'one of the many modes through which Lessing deliber-
ately distances herself from English tradition, implicitly
defines that tradition as insular and unusable in the post-
World War II period'.[7] Those favoured writers are also
male. Lessing's gender preference takes the place of the
male pseudonym. No longer needing to claim a male name,
as countless women writers had a century and less earlier
(including her heroine, Olive Schreiner), Lessing nonetheless confronts a male literary establishment in mid-twen-
tieth-century Britain. Thus, she empowers herself with
male, non-British, literary ancestors.

Lessing's pantheon also testifies to the literary prefer-
ences of European intellectuals, many of them Commu-
nists, who had fled Europe as Hitler came to power and
made their way to Southern Africa. Through their influence and her autodidactism, Lessing shaped herself as an
intellectual. I stress the self-shaping because her formal

schooling was minimal and, by all accounts, dismal. That schooling followed an English model with the 7-year-old Doris Taylor sent to board at the Roman Catholic Convent in Salisbury for a five-year term. A one-year stint at the Girls' High School in Salisbury capped Lessing's formal schooling; she left school at 14, much to the annoyance of her mother who had musical aspirations for her daughter. Perhaps the best record of Lessing's schooling is found in the broad biographical stroke in *Martha Quest* with Martha's rejection of exams and indoctrination in favour of reading and self-empowerment. Like Lessing, Martha finds two texts of supreme importance: the landscape and the novel.

Discussing *Martha Quest* in *Tradition and Dream*, Walter Allen makes an interesting comparison between Lessing and George Eliot, a comparison that I want to extend to Lessing's biography, but first Allen's observation:

> In the passionate seriousness of her response to life Martha Quest is in the direct line of descent from Maggie Tulliver, and Doris Lessing shows her [own] kinship to George Eliot both in her technique here and in her sober, unsentimental scrutiny of behaviour, motives and morals.[8]

I agree with Allen's view of the kinship in the novels; in fact I would extend the argument for kinship to the writers' biographies and to their empowerment as intellectuals. Deirdre David notes that Eliot consciously made herself an intellectual:

> Her career is a narrative of self-creation, the story of a powerfully intelligent woman graced with an impressive ability to discipline and expand her intellect through sustained scholarly study. To the end of her writing life,

Eliot directed her comprehensive mind across a wide scope of cultural, social, scientific, and political thought.[9]

I want to argue that Lessing's is also 'a narrative of self-creation'.

Custom and a century separate George Eliot and Doris Lessing, and earlier I quoted one of Lessing's several appraisals of Eliot: 'George Eliot is good as far as she goes.' I ascribe the dismissive note in that judgement to anxiety of influence, the younger, colonial newcomer going up against the established cultural icon (another mother–daughter battle in Lessing). Despite Lessing's dismissal, the similarities in their struggles toward self-creation are real and intriguing. Neither woman is a product of the university: Eliot cannot enter, Lessing will not enter. Both women are largely self-taught through voracious reading; both find intellectual support in a circle of radical friends: Eliot at *The Westminster Review* in London, Lessing in communist study groups in Salisbury. At odds with the values of their families, Eliot and Lessing move through radical politics to conservative foundationalism: Eliot moving from free thinking toward the mysticism she approaches in *Daniel Deronda* (1876), Lessing moving from Communism to Sufism beginning with *Landlocked* (1965). And as Claire Sprague notes in a comparison of *Middlemarch* and *The Golden Notebook*, both writers while often critical of feminist movements write novels which 'nonetheless constantly undercut or struggle against "hierarchy and containment"'.[10] Finally, Eliot and Lessing become sybil figures for many of their readers.

But before Lessing became a sybil she had to become a writer. After the close of her formal education, Lessing began her writing career on the family farm, an apprenticeship that ended when at about 18 she left the isolation of the countryside to pursue something of a career in Salisbury as a telephone operator and office clerk. Daytime activity, however, was distinctly inferior to the social activities linking her first to the smart young people in Salisbury, captured forever in the banal horrors of the Sports Club sequences in *Children of Violence*, and then with European immigrants and RAF members who were making their way to Southern Rhodesia because of impending war. From the first group Lessing secured a husband, Frank Charles Wisdom, who was in the civil service. Lessing married in 1939, bore two children, and divorced in 1943.

From the second group, the British and European outsiders in the colony, Lessing secured a political education. *A Proper Marriage*, *A Ripple from the Storm* (1958), and *The Golden Notebook* (1962) capture some of the exhaustion and exhilaration of endless debate in ever-changing study groups devoted to radical politics committed to obliterating the colour bar. Lessing acquired an intense education in the nature of political organisation, an education often at odds with the education in timelessness provided by the natural setting of her father's farm. Yet even in this activist stage, Lessing's attraction to timeless moments manifests itself as early as *Martha Quest* and *Landlocked*. Action and reflection compete with one another in Lessing's fiction and in her life.

That competition may have intensified Lessing's desire to leave the Far Counties behind her. The psychological, emotional, and intellectual overload of the war years in Salisbury led Lessing to think of emigration to England, for, as she observed in 1957, 'England seems to me the ideal country to live in because it is quiet and unstimulating and leaves you in peace.'[11] Ironically, this 'expert in unsettlement' as Lorna Sage aptly terms Lessing sought a more settled world.[12] Taking her young son from her second marriage to Gottfried Lessing, whom she married in 1944 and divorced in 1949, she reversed her parents'

pattern and left the Far Counties for the Home Counties in
1949. Lessing brought with her a typescript of *The Grass Is
Singing* and secured a publisher, Michael Joseph, who
issued the work in 1950. Through this much-celebrated
first novel (seven reprints in five months), Lessing realised
her long-imagined vocation, for as she told Roy Newquist
in 1964: 'I wrote some bad novels in my teens. I always
knew I would be a writer, but not until I was quite old – 26
or 7 – did I realise I'd better stop saying I was *going* to be
one and get down to business' (SPV, p. 46). Lessing got
down to business with *The Grass Is Singing*.

2 Two Versions of a White African Girlhood: *The Grass Is Singing* and *Children of Violence*

During the voyage over, the girl had read *The Story of a South African Farm* and this had begun an intellectual revolution in her.

(RS, p. 202)

Thus, the narrator of the third volume in *Children of Violence* describes Olive Schreiner's influence on the intellectual life of Mrs Van der Blyt, a courageous and admired Afrikaner liberal. Schreiner's influence can also be traced in the intellectual life of Doris Lessing who in her 'Afterword to *The Story of an African Farm*' writes:

I read the novel when I was fourteen or so; understanding very well the isolation described in it; responding to her sense of Africa the magnificent – mine, and everyone's who knows Africa; realising that this was one of the few rare books. For it is in that small number of novels, with *Moby Dick*, *Jude the Obscure*, *Wuthering Heights*, perhaps one or two others, which is on a frontier of the human mind. Also, this was the first 'real' book I'd met with that had Africa for a setting.

Here was the substance of truth, and not from England
or Russia or France or America, necessitating all kinds
of mental translations, switches, correspondences, but
reflecting what I knew and could see. And the book
became part of me, as the few rare books do.

(SPV, pp. 98–9)

There is much in the quotation to which I want to return
in this chapter, but at this stage I want to focus on
Schreiner as something of a presiding genius in Lessing's
maturation novels. That, in fact, the struggle Lyndall faces
in Schreiner's novel is reflected in the struggles faced by
Mary Turner in *The Grass Is Singing* and by Martha Quest
in the *Children of Violence* series, especially in *Martha
Quest* and in *Landlocked* (1945).

Schreiner and Lessing were political activists and critics
of their respective colonial societies, nineteenth-century
South Africa and twentieth-century Rhodesia, who began
their literary careers in England. Both published first
novels there, *The Story of an African Farm* (1883) and
The Grass is Singing (Lessing's own story of an African
farm), that won them a fair amount of celebrity and
financial success. Both novels depict what for a largely
British reading public, whether in nineteenth or twentieth
centuries, would be labelled an exotic locale – a white
outpost in a remote colony. Both novels also dramatically
focus, Lessing's more singularly than Schreiner's, on a
woman's failed attempt to battle with the colonial society's – for them the world's – attempt to tell 'us what we are
to be'.[1]

Since its publication, *The Grass Is Singing* has been read
as social critique, mythic novel, romance, and detective
story. I want to read it as a *Bildungsroman*, a maturation
novel albeit a limited one, and concentrate on the development of the female protagonist, Mary Turner, whose
murder is discovered and dispatched in Chapter One.

That dispatch by the colonial society involves a speedy trial of the 'native', who according to the newspaper account that opens the book is presumed to have been 'in search of valuables' (GS, p. 1). Moses, the native, is never named in the account. Even more expeditious in settling the issue of the murder is the silence with which the white community robes the event: 'For they did not discuss the murder; that was the most extraordinary thing about it. It was as if they had a sixth sense which told them everything there was to be known, although the three people in a position to explain the facts said nothing' (GS, pp. 1–2). Such silence is particularly interesting since that same community is later depicted as thriving on the quirks of the Turners who 'for years . . . had provided the staple of gossip among the farmers round about' (GS, p. 197). After the murder, the settler wagons are brought into a circle by Charlie Slatter, an avaricious and successful farmer, and the enemy – curiosity about the relationship between a white 'missus' and her black servant – is kept at bay. Everything is quickly and neatly closed and everyone silenced – except for the unidentified, omniscient narrator who proceeds to explore Mary's life and to track her psychological deterioration.

Let me note that authorial omniscience in *The Grass Is Singing* is limited to white characters, particularly Mary and Dick Turner. No attempt is made to explain Moses's psychology. He is a type, the ever-threatening and beckoning black man who comes to dominate even Mary's dreams: 'On each occasion in her dream he had stood over her, powerful and commanding, yet kind, but forcing her into a position where she had to touch him' (GS, p. 181). Lorna Sage has commented on the problem Moses's limited characterisation presents:

To explain Moses, to write him out, might well be to *white* him out, even if one did it very differently from the newspaper clipping's account of the thieving houseboy. But then again, to leave him blank, in a book so conscious of the oppressive function of silence, is deeply embarrassing. What this dilemma reveals is a vital problem in Lessing's writing. How much can one represent? How much, that is, can one find others in oneself, in experience, imagination, and language? In short, though on a different level, Lessing the writer is encountering her settlers' problem and hasn't found a solution.[2]

The same problem intrigues Ruth Whittaker in *Doris Lessing* where she argues that Moses 'remains a cypher rather than a character whose personality and motivation we can understand'.[3] But Whittaker goes on to give an absolution of sorts when she notes:

> Mrs. Lessing's least successful short stories are where she attempts to write from the point of view of black Africans, and perhaps one has to accept the difficulty, if not the impossibility of such a task without feeling guilty of an apartheid of the imagination.[4]

Lessing's bind is neither more nor less the problem of any writer who tries to imagine the other.

Schreiner was not any more successful; her kaffirs are part of the locale in *The Story of an African Farm*, no more than that. Both Schreiner and Lessing present the stories of white African girlhoods in their fiction. Read as social critique which the original title *Black and White* surely invites,[5] *The Grass Is Singing* offers a limited analysis of what the colonial system has wrought on marginal white settlers, like the Turners.[6] When it comes to the natives and the landscape, social realism gives way to a romanticism that actually recolonises the natives, particularly

Moses. Lessing presents him as a sexual energy rather than as a person; he is a black Heathcliff deprived of any personal history.

It is, however, the novel as *Bildungsroman* or maturation narrative that interests me here, especially the extent to which Mary Turner is shaped by nature and by nurture, what Olive Schreiner observed as the ends which the world sets before young girls. Social determinism, a major element in *The Story of an African Farm*, dominates *The Grass Is Singing*. Spending a horrid childhood in a dusty dorp overshadowed by 'the store', Mary quickly learns to reject the other, here embodied in 'the little Greek girl whom she was not allowed to play with, because her mother said her parents were dagoes' (GS, p. 30). She also learns to shun her own sexuality as she watches the disastrous marriage of her drunken father and embittered mother. Only the prospect of education presents a possibility of escape for Mary. 'Then she was sent to boarding school and her life changed. She was extremely happy, so happy that she dreaded going home at holiday times. . .' (GS, p. 32). So happy at school, Mary tries to remain a schoolgirl forever; ironically her very obsession with escaping the life of her parents traps her in a similar life.

I use the word obsession because Lessing presents a pathology more than a maturation process in her characterisation of Mary who seems more mature as a young girl than she does as a young woman. One great difference between Lessing's Mary and Schreiner's Lyndall is choice shaped by analysis. For all her vagueness, Lyndall tries to move beyond her own experience and to analyse her situation; Mary Turner, short on reflection, is ever reacting. Despite the blurb on the Plume paperback edition of *The Grass Is Singing* which argues that 'We watch the heroine, Mary Turner, deteriorate from a self-confident, independent young woman into the depressed, frustrated

wife of an ineffectual, unsuccessful farmer', I contend that
Mary is never self-confident and never independent (unless
earning one's living is the sole measure of independence).

Mary, strangely described by the narrator as an inheri-
tor of her mother's 'arid feminism' (GS, p. 33), is stunted
by her very limited capacity for self-analysis; nothing in the
narrative suggests that Mary's happy school-days offered
her models of thought. She is never shown as having any
intellectual curiosity. For a time she is able to resist the life
of her parents through work. Almost a century after
Lyndall's inability to forge an independent economic
existence in *The Story of an African Farm*, Mary Turner
can find work as a secretary and do well; at 30:

> She was by now the personal secretary of her employer,
> and was earning good money. If she had wanted, she
> could have taken a flat and lived the smart sort of life.
> She was quite presentable. She had the undistinguished,
> dead-level appearance of South African white democ-
> racy. Her voice was one of thousands: flattened, a little
> sing-song, clipped. Anyone could have worn her clothes.
> There was nothing to prevent her living by herself, even
> running her own car, entertaining on a small scale. *She
> could have become a person on her own account. But this
> was against her instinct.*
>
> (GS, pp. 34–5) (italics mine)

Mary remains a 16-year-old locked away in a girls' club,
'And she still wore her hair little-girl fashion on her
shoulders, and wore little-girl frocks in pastel colors, and
kept her shy, naive manner' (GS, p. 37). Through work
and a strange impersonality, Mary instinctively resists
what her world requires – marriage. That resistance,
however, is never accompanied by analysis or reflection.
Soon enough overheard gossip, ironic in light of the silence

that attends her murder, pressures Mary into a breakdown and an arid marriage to Dick Turner, a farmer with dreams and no practical sense.

Presenting Mary as victim, Lessing never grants her even the glimmer of an intellectual life so that Mary becomes more and more trapped in a physical world that frees her dream life and challenges her sexuality, a challenge extensively and erotically dramatised in her relationship with Moses.

> he forced her, now, to treat him as a human being; it was impossible for her to thrust him out of her mind like something unclean, as she had done with all others in the past. She was being forced into contact, and she never ceased to be aware of him. She realized, daily, that there was something in it that was dangerous, but what it was she was unable to define.
>
> (GS, p. 181)

Without a capacity for analysis, 'she was unable to define' since nothing in her experience nor in her limited learning has given her any means of definition. Nor can Mary work through her dreams to clearer understanding of herself and her situation.

Later in her career, Lessing used the dream as a way to understanding;[7] in *The Grass Is Singing*, especially in Mary's dreams of Moses and her father, the dream is a way of heightening the character's psychological terror. Once again, Mary is acted upon. This story of an African girlhood ends with collective and individual failure. Not so Lessing's next version of a white African girlhood in *Martha Quest*.

Once more, I want to invoke Olive Schreiner and *The Story of an African Farm* as a way of reading Lessing. Earlier, I noted that Lyndall's struggle to escape the farm,

to secure some self-ownership, finds a reflection in the
struggles of Mary Turner (a struggle limited by Mary's
pathology) and Martha Quest. Lyndall's struggle certainly
informs *Martha Quest*, with Martha seeking intellectual,
sexual, and political ends much like those unsuccessfully
sought by Lyndall. But other ends also inform *Martha
Quest* and add to its complexity. To begin to explain that
complexity, I want to turn to another character in *The
Story of an African Farm*. Let me do that by way of
another of Lessing's observations in her 'Afterword to
The Story of an African Farm':

> Lyndall and Waldo: Olive said that in these two she had
> put herself. They share a soul; and when Lyndall dies,
> Waldo has to die. But it is Waldo who is the heart of the
> book, a ragged, sullen, clumsy farm boy, all inarticulate
> hunger – not for education, like Lyndall, but for the
> unknown. And it is to Waldo that Olive gave the chapter
> that is the core, not only of this novel, but of all her
> work. It is called 'Waldo's Stranger' . . .
>
> (SPV, p. 105)

Lessing then goes on to describe the legend of the Hunter
in Schreiner's novel.

Lessing wrote her 'Afterword' for a 1968 reissue of *The
Story of an African Farm*, a time when she was completing
The Children of Violence series. In rereading Schreiner,
Lessing was also discovering a way to explain the turn in
her own work from the realism of *Martha Quest* to the
mixed form of *The Four-Gated City* (1969), a turn from the
known to the unknown. I realise that I am making a claim
that cannot be fully supported until I discuss *The Four-
Gated City* in a succeeding chapter but let me begin to
support my claim with *Martha Quest*.

The novel opens with the 15-year-old Martha, a self-
exile on her father's farm, reading Havelock Ellis and

bored with the presence of her mother and Mrs Van
Rensberg, a neighbour. Intellectually nurtured by books
supplied by the Cohen brothers, sons of the Jewish shop-
keeper in the area, Martha establishes herself as the other
vis-à-vis her parents and the settler community, whether
British or Afrikaner. She is at war with everyone, even
herself; reading Havelock Ellis in the presence of two
women who, from Martha's view, should be appalled by
his ideas, leads to self-defeat:

> Just as Mrs Quest found it necessary to protest at half-
> hourly intervals, that Martha would get sunstroke if she
> did not come into the shade, so she eventually remarked
> that she supposed it did no harm for girls to read that
> sort of book; and once again Martha directed towards
> them a profoundly scornful glare, which was also
> unhappy and exasperated; for she felt that in some
> contradictory way she had been driven to use this book
> as a means of asserting herself, and now found the
> weapon had gone limp and useless in her hands.
>
> (MQ, p. 4)

The narrative is made up of a series of unsuccessful
assaults by Martha on established pieties; yet more often
than not assertion leads to exasperation in *Martha Quest*.

Her battle against her parents, especially against her
mother, leads to the city and to the illusion of independence when she secures a job in a lawyer's office. (The
paternal not the maternal figure offers what little support
Martha receives throughout *Children of Violence*.) Seemingly free from familial constraints, Martha experiences
the heady air of sexual liberation and political awakening,
but I stress 'seemingly' because all roads ultimately lead
back to the constraints represented by her parents' marriage when Martha out of boredom and lack of anything
better to do marries Douglas Knowell at the end of the

novel. Early in the novel the narrator, describing the ebb and flow in the relationship between Mrs Quest and Mrs Van Rensberg notes 'Everything would continue as usual, in fact' (MQ, p. 7). The same matter-of-fact pronouncement can be made about Martha Quest's life at the end of the first volume of *Children of Violence* if one looks at the known world of the novel.

What I want to chart, however, is another terrain – what Lessing when writing of Schreiner called the unknown – that is but momentarily glimpsed by Martha and by the reader. That terrain was walked earlier by Waldo in *The Story of an African Farm*; meeting his stranger, Waldo hears that 'All true facts of nature or the mind are related.'[8] He is given a way of connecting seen and unseen worlds; much of Martha's estrangement has to do with not being able to make that connection or Lessing's inability to give her allegorical bent as full a play as Schreiner was prepared to do. Given her own intellectual history and the dramatic autodidactism that centred it, Lessing would naturally turn to the nineteenth-century realism in the form of the *Bildungsroman*. The form, however, proves inadequate for what she wants. The very constraints of the realistic form that Lessing chooses for the first three volumes of *Children of Violence* work against the unknown because the form celebrates an empirical world that can be known and mastered.

Both Schreiner and Lessing try to assuage 'immortal longings' in a realistic form that cannot adequately accommodate such fulfilment. For, as George Levine argues:

Traditionally realism is associated with determinism. The anti-romance is the denial of the imagination's power to control circumstance. And thus the characteristic subject of realistic fiction is the contest between dream and reality; the characteristic progress, disenchantment. The single character is implicated in a world of the contingent and must make peace with society and nature or be destroyed.[9]

Schreiner seems to endorse 'the denial of the imagination's power' in her 1883 'Preface' to the second edition of *The Story of an African Farm* when she sets up a division between the 'brilliant phases and shapes which the imagination sees in far-off lands' which the realistic writer must reject. 'Sadly he must squeeze the colours from his brush, and dip it into the gray pigments around him. He must paint what lies before him.'[10]

On the surface, both Schreiner and Lessing paint what lies before them; yet neither writer finally denies the imagination's power in her narrative. Both writers expand their realistic forms[11] to accommodate imagination through what Nancy Bazin in her work on Lessing calls 'the moment of revelation'.[12] For Schreiner there is more than one 'moment of revelation' in *The Story of an African Farm*; indeed Waldo's frequent communion with nature testifies to his unarticulated connection with an 'unseen world', and finally, his dialogue with the stranger and the Hunter's allegory suggests the existence of a community of seers who possess received wisdom. No such community is suggested in *Martha Quest* where the 'moment of revelation' is a lengthy but single experience early in the novel.

Walking home alone Martha finds herself in 'intense, joyful melancholy' (MQ, pp. 51–2) and discovers:

what was futile was her own idea of herself and her place in the chaos of matter. What was demanded of her was that she should accept something quite different; it was as if something new was demanding conception, with her flesh as host; as if there were a necessity, which she must bring herself to accept, that she should allow herself to dissolve and be formed by that necessity. But it did not last; the force desisted, and left her

standing on the road, already trying to reach out after 'the
moment' so that she might retain its message from the
wasting and creating chaos of darkness.

(MQ, p. 53)

Martha's spiritual experience leaves her looking for words
to describe it and her problem with the limitation of
language foreshadows Lessing's more elaborate statement
of the problem in *Briefing for a Descent into Hell* (1971).

More than that, however, her experience leaves her
apparently unchanged, a view that Nancy Bazin would
oppose. Bazin argues that Martha's experience early in the
novel leads to her developing 'a double self, with one self
observing the other critically'.[13] But that doubleness is
there from the opening pages of the novel. My reading of
the 'moment of revelation' is that the episode is a lacuna in
the *Bildungsroman* format that Lessing uses in *Children of
Violence* at least until *The Four-Gated City* where the last
half of the text is given over to the mature Martha's doing
what the teenaged Martha cannot do: accepting 'something quite different'.

On one level, the Martha of *Martha Quest*, *A Proper
Marriage*, and *A Ripple from the Storm* accepts 'something
quite different' as she moves from farm to town, from the
values of the Sports Club to the values of the Communist
Party. But 'the something quite different' that precipitates
the epiphany early in *Martha Quest* points to a level other
than the political and social – 'the something new . . .
[that] was demanding conception' (MQ, p. 53) cannot be
realised in the bustle of activity to which Martha seems
committed. Indeed much of Martha's busyness is accompanied by a lassitude, a world-weariness that speaks to a
division in her between the demands of the known world –
Martha as modern young woman, marrying, having a
child, having affairs, becoming politically active, divor-
cing, etc. – and her psycho-spiritual state – best caught in

the periods of illness and times of yearning for illness. Nowhere is that yearning more clearly evident than in *A Ripple from the Storm*, the third and most politically engaged volume of the series. In the midst of endless meetings of the band of comrades, Martha is divided between her desire to act and be politically correct and her recognition

> that it would be pleasant to be ill for a day or two, to have time to think, and even – this last thought gave her a severe spasm of guilt – to be alone for a little, not always to be surrounded by people.
>
> (RS, p. 93)

I do not want to minimize the importance of politics in *Children of Violence*, a ground that has been well-covered in Lessing criticism. However, the 'something quite different' that the teenaged Martha cannot accept is not a new political and social order: rather it is a new psychological-spiritual order which the older Martha begins to grasp in *Landlocked*, which Lessing begins with an epigraph from Idries Shah:

> The Mulla walked into a shop one day. The owner came forward to serve him.
> 'First things first,' said Nasrudin, 'did you see me walk into your shop?'
> 'Of course.'
> 'Have you ever seen me before?'
> 'Never in my life.'
> 'Then how do you know it is me?'
>
> (L, p. 275)

The Mulla's final question emphasises what has been an increasing concern through the series, the question of identity and its cognate the relationship between the individual and the community or collective. And certainly on one level the query is asked and answered realistically. Martha Quest tries on a variety of clothes and roles – daughter, typist, lover, wife, mother, political activist, etc. – in her attempt to answer the question and in an attempt to place herself in a community. But as early as *Martha Quest* lacunae disrupt the realistic narrative to suggest that the question must be asked and answered on some other level.

In *Landlocked*, Lessing begins to explore that different level. The sources of her epigraphs reflect the difference: two of the epigraphs are drawn from Sufi parables and one from St Polycarp, replacing the literary sources – like Proust, Turgenev, Lewis Carroll, and Olive Schreiner – favoured in earlier volumes. In the narrative itself that different level is explored in the curious relationship between Martha Quest and Thomas Stern, a Polish Jew. Unhappily married to the repressed and repressive Anton Hesse, Martha Quest begins an affair with the married Thomas Stern who works as a gardener. But I have used the word curious to describe the relationship and so far have presented a fairly standard extra-marital relationship which in one way captures the involvement between Martha and Thomas who share not only sexual but also political passions, Martha's for Communism and Thomas's for Zionism.

The curious character of their relationship, however, does not lie in the sexual or political levels of their involvement. The most interesting energy between Martha and Thomas connects to 'something quite different', to something that cannot be contained in political or sexual arrangements. While linked to the known world through his past as victimised European Jew and through his commitment to the establishment of a Zionist state, Thomas is an enigmatic figure in the novel who acts almost on a par with Waldo's 'stranger' in *The Story of an African Farm*. He brings gnomic messages to Martha.

Two striking examples of Thomas as spiritual guide, as teacher, are worth examining.

Early in Part Two, Thomas and Martha are in their 'bower of bliss', the loft in his brother's garden shed that 'had become her home' (L, p. 387) when Thomas notes:

the city isn't important, not really. The big city's not been with us long enough to be important, we are already beyond it. Because now we think: that star over there, that star's got a different time-scale from us. We are born under that star and make love under it and put our children to sleep under it and are buried under it. The elm tree is out of date, it's had its day. Now we try all the time, day and night, to understand: that star has a different time-scale, we are like midges compared to the star. And that's why you're all on edge and why I'm sick although I'm a peasant from Sochaczen.

(L, p. 386)

Belief in the city, the collective, fuels the realistic level of *Landlocked* where Martha, Mrs Van, Jasmine Cohen, Johnny Lindsay and others fight for various versions of a new, more just community. Belief in the city, a new Jerusalem, fuels Thomas Stern's willingness to fight for Israel. But those beliefs that dominate most of the narrative are questioned in the loft as Thomas talks cryptically and parabolically of 'a different time scale'.

By the end of *Landlocked* Thomas Stern has died in a remote African village far from the promised land and Martha Quest, finally divorced from Anton, awaits clearance for emigration to England and the Home Counties. The collective to which Martha has been connected has all but dissolved through the death, exile, emigration, or aging of its members. Martha's final role is to act as editor of Johnny Lindsay's realistic memoir and Thomas's strange 'last testament':

One version consisted of the short biographies and the
obituaries and the recipes and the charms and the tales
and the anecdotes. The other, typed out on flimsy sheets
which could be inserted over the heavier sheets of the
first version, made a whole roughly like the original –
more or less common sense, as a foundation, with a
layer of nonsense over it.

(L, pp. 535–6)

Lindsay's memoir is easy enough to transcribe and to leave
behind. Thomas's narrative while frustrating and unclear
is the text Martha carries with her to England. It is a
narrative that might be described as Lessing described *The
Story of an African Farm*, a narrative 'on a frontier of the
human mind', the only frontier that remains worth the
crossing for exiles like Martha Quest and Doris Lessing.

3 The Sex War: *Martha Quest, A Proper Marriage,* and *The Golden Notebook*

The truth is I have sympathy for men. Men ought to be horizon-bashing, challenging and raising hell. A woman would be perfectly happy with that sort of man.

Doris Lessing, 1969[1]

I've never agreed that the women's movement should be restricted to women, . . . I didn't expect much to arise out of it, and nothing much has.

Doris Lessing, 1984[2]

Despite Lessing's sometime claim to being one, feminist is not a term that I can easily apply to her. I cannot imagine Lessing endorsing arguments about difference or calls for separatism. The doctrinaire quality of so much contemporary feminism would be unappealing to the Lessing who wrote *The Four-Gated City* and *Canopus in Argos: Archives.* That same doctrinaire quality would be equally unappealing to the Lessing who wrote the early volumes of *Children of Violence* and *The Golden Notebook.* Still those earlier books present female protagonists living in societies grappling with what the Victorians called 'the Woman

Question'. And like so many of the Victorian reformers before her, Lessing centres her response to 'the Woman Question' on a critique of the institution of marriage which she vigorously attacks in *Martha Quest* and *A Proper Marriage*. In both novels, Lessing presents a critique of marriage and family as the enemy of free women.

As I noted in the preceding chapter, Martha Quest, like Mary Turner in *The Grass Is Singing*, thinks she can escape her parents' life and the entrapment of marriage. She desperately wants to resist her mother's choices so she escapes to the city and the life of an independent, modern woman. The world lies before her or so she thinks. Lessing, however, is too shrewd an observer of human beings and society to ignore the effects of nurture. Martha carries her mother's values with her and soon enough marriage makes its claim. Ironically, Martha's initial attraction to Douglas Knowell results from a misperception: 'he was so different from the Sports Club men!' (MQ, p. 216). For a time she sees him as one of the 'horizon-bashing, challenging men' Doris Lessing later praised in 1969. That misperception gives way quickly enough, but she cannot act on her recognition: 'She did not understand him. She looked at him, bewildered. Also, she was disgusted and impatient. Her own body was aching, even her shoulders ached, and her breasts felt arrogant and chilled. But she was bound to love him, that claim had been laid on her' (MQ, p. 221).

Time and again in *Martha Quest*, Martha recognises something intellectually about her role as woman but does not act on the recognition. The most dramatic instance of Martha's inability to act comes at the end of *Martha Quest* after a political argument with Douglas:

> She said to herself that now she could free herself, she need not marry him; at the same time, she knew quite well she would marry him; she could not help it; she was

being dragged towards it, whether she liked it or not.
She also heard a voice remarking calmly within her that
she would not stay married to him; but this voice had no
time to make itself heard before he turned to her, and
asked again, this time quietly and pleasantly, for his
anger had subsided, whether she wanted to change her
mind. She replied that she did not.

(MQ, p. 243)

Indeed, Lessing's centring on Martha's consciousness
reveals that Martha is shaped by more than one fate: a
recognisable social pressure to marry ('she was being
dragged toward it') and an unspecified power that suggests future action ('this voice had no time to make itself
heard'). That voice, however, becomes much more audible,
even deafening, in *A Proper Marriage.*

The novel records the breakdown of the Knowell
marriage and Martha's growing preoccupation with politics, a preoccupation central to both *A Ripple from the
Storm* and *Landlocked.* Most significantly, *A Proper
Marriage* is Lessing's most lacerating portrait of a marriage.[3] She elaborately explores Martha's attitudes towards
and dramatic rejection of the conventional woman's mission, the role of wife and mother. The rejection is so
complete, replete with scenes of domestic violence, that I
read the novel as the work in which Lessing, as Woolf
earlier, kills 'the Angel of the House'.

On the surface, Martha's generation has much more
freedom than her mother's generation. An urban setting
provides stimuli that the veld could not; it is a world of
constant social activity. Sex manuals and discussions of
sexual practices seem to have overcome Victorian prudery.
Domestic work is taken care of by invisible blacks,[4] and a
husband in the Civil Service makes work as a secretary
unnecessary. But being a modern woman causes its own
peculiar problems for the newly married Martha:

And now the question of work fronted her. She had
understood she was not alone in her position of a woman who disdained both housework and a 'job', but was
vaguely expected by her husband–but only because of
her own insistence on it–to be engaged in work of her
own. Both Stella and Alice had claimed the state.
Martha had heard their respective husbands speak of
them in precisely the same tone of pride and satisfaction
that Douglas used to her. Their wives were not as those
of other men.

                                        (PM, pp. 62–3)

Neither domestic nor office work actually appeals to
Martha, but as a modern woman, one for whom 'the
Woman Question' seems to have been answered, she can
claim some work. Or perhaps more specific to Lessing, she
must be claimed by it: 'it was ten in the morning, and her
day was her own. Her work was free to start when it
would' (PM, p. 64).

As in *Martha Quest*, the Martha of *A Proper Marriage* is
far more acted upon than acting; with plenty of leisure she
has no idea of how to use it. Marriage has turned Martha
into the Sleeping Beauty; the prince's kiss has imprisoned
not freed her. A proper marriage has turned her into
property, a transformation which she recognises:

'Well, Matty, and now you'll be free to get on with your
own work.'
It was with these words that Douglas dropped his
parting kiss on her cheek when he left for the office
each morning, and with a look of pure satisfaction. The
kindly, confident young man crossed the untidy bedroom towards the door, bouncing a little from the balls
of his feet, smiling backwards at Martha, who was
sitting in a tangle of crumpled and stained silk in a
mess of bedclothes, and vanished whistling down the

corridor. The gleam of proprietary satisfaction never failed to arouse in Martha a flush of strong resentment, which was as unfailingly quenched by a succeeding guilt.

(PM, p. 60)

Not even pregnancy can bring Martha out of her vagueness. Trying to conform to another set of social claims, those attached to maternity, deepens Martha's estrangement. Lessing is merciless in presenting dehumanised medical practice in her scenes of Martha in childbirth. Only the presence of a kindly black cleaning woman who helps Martha during labour breaks the sterility of her experience. Here and elsewhere in *A Proper Marriage* the intuitive acceptance of black women is contrasted with the excessive self-awareness of white women, presumably in favour of black women. Here and elsewhere, Martha's (Lessing's) version of 'the noble savage' produces its own discomfort.[5]

Motherhood only intensifies Martha's estrangement. Caroline, Martha's daughter, plays the role of double and rival to her mother. On the one hand, Caroline secures the love and acceptance from Mrs Quest that Martha never realises in her relationship with her mother. On the other hand, Caroline embodies the potential which Martha at 21 feels she has squandered in marriage. Indeed, the hours alone with Caroline provide a strange stimulus to Martha's imagination as she begins to break through her own vagueness to an understanding of her situation:

'Two years ago, I was free as air. I could have done anything, been anything. Because the essence of the daydreams of every girl who isn't married is just that: it's the only time they are more free than men. Men *have* to be something, but you'll find when you grow up, my poor child, that you'll see yourself as a ballet dancer, or

a business executive, or the wife of a Prime Minister, or
the mistress of somebody important, or even at extreme
moments a nun or a missionary. You'll imagine yourself
doing all sorts of things in all sorts of countries; the
point is, your will will be your limit. Anything'll be
possible. But you will not see yourself sitting in a small
room bound for twenty-four hours of the day–with
years of it in front of you–to a small child.'

(PM, p. 205)

In the preceding excerpt, Martha presumes a freedom ('I
was free as air. I could have done anything, been anything.') that never existed; she has little or no training to
have 'been anything'. Neither in *A Proper Marriage* nor
elsewhere in *Children of Violence* does Lessing present
Martha with any real interest in being something, in
having some sort of professional identity. Interestingly
enough, Martha's own imagining about lost freedom does
not preclude marriage as a choice ('the wife of a Prime
Minister'); it just precludes a proper marriage to a dullard
like Douglas and a life of predictable security. The right
man or a 'real man' is part of the Lessing emotional
landscape in *Children of Violence* and in *The Golden
Notebook*. In fact, throughout much of *Children of Violence*, Martha defines herself in relationship to men; time
and again as with her relationship with Anton in *A Ripple
from the Storm*, Martha waits for a man 'to create her into
something new' (RS, p. 155).

Nothing new seems possible, however, in *A Proper
Marriage* Her experience with Caroline, the war which
takes Douglas to another part of the colony and brings in
British soldiers, and her own growing political awareness
lead finally to Martha's recognition that 'She did not feel
like Douglas's wife or Caroline's mother' (PM, p. 250).
That recognition precipitates not just angry exchanges but
also domestic violence which Lessing describes most

effectively. Finally, at considerable cost, Martha secures her way out of a proper marriage.

It is one thing though to divorce and to surrender custody, quite another to recognise what she does feel like, what to do next. Martha does not make this recognition in any of the volumes of *Children of Violence*. Neither frantic political activity, nor passionate love affairs; neither notoriety as one of the colony's Reds nor anonymity as colonial in England lead to Martha's recognising what she would be. While she repudiates the domestic caretaker role in *A Proper Marriage*, she finds herself playing this role time and again in *Children of Violence*, most dramatically in *The Four-Gated City*.

Martha constantly gives in to the claims of others and has little or nothing to show as the fruit of her labour. She produces nothing. This, I think, has to do with Lessing's much greater interest in process rather than in product although as Jenny Taylor argues 'the *Children of Violence* sequence describes a process, though it's presented as a product'.[6] In 'The Small Personal Voice', Lessing describes her plan for *Children of Violence*, two volumes of which had been published when she wrote the essay, as 'a study of the individual conscience in its relations to the collective' (SPV, p. 14). But more and more in the novel sequence, as I noted in Chapter 2, Lessing emphasises universality rather than individuality. By the publication of *The Four-Gated City*, a novel which I will discuss in the next chapter, the emphasis on individual action has disappeared in favour of the presentation of the transpersonal. But even by the time of *A Proper Marriage* individual action seems of limited value as Martha responds as much as she acts: 'Martha went home with the feeling that she had accomplished another stage in that curious process which would set her free' (PM, p. 339). The 'curious process' becomes more and more intriguing as Lessing writes the remaining volumes of

Children of Violence, and her essentialism becomes more pronounced.

In the midst of composing *Children of Violence*, Lessing wrote her most-celebrated novel, *The Golden Notebook*, in 1962. For readers – especially women – then and now, the novel has been seen as Margaret Drabble observes 'as a book about Women's Liberation, and with good cause'.[7] Lessing has a different view. Nine years after publishing the novel, Lessing wrote a much-cited 'Preface' in which she described *The Golden Notebook*'s being 'instantly belittled, by friendly reviewers as well as by hostile ones, as being about the sex war, or was claimed by women as a useful weapon in the sex war' (GN, viii). Lessing goes on to avow her commitment to women's rights in terms that a Victorian could endorse and then moves away from the topic to what for her are the more significant issues of her 'Preface'. What she does in her 'Preface' is what she does elsewhere – she marginalises 'the Woman Question' and clothes it in the quaint phrase 'sex war'; one instantly thinks of *Lysistrata* and D. H. Lawrence. In 'The Small Personal Voice', published five years before *The Golden Notebook*, Lessing criticises John Osborne's *Look Back in Anger*: 'But when it reaches the point where we are offered the sex war as a serious substitute for social struggle, even if ironically, then it is time to examine the reasons' (SPV, p. 19). Again, the dismissal.

Despite Lessing's statements, the most recent American paperback edition of *The Golden Notebook* underscores the novel's power over women readers when it quotes from Elizabeth Hardwick's review for *The New York Times*. According to Hardwick, '*The Golden Notebook* is Doris Lessing's most important work and has left its mark upon the ideas and feelings of a whole generation of women.' Hardwick's view is supported by a variety of reader responses; let me cite but two. In the collection *Notebooks/Memoirs/Archives*, Jean McCrindle and Elizabeth

Wilson write of reading *The Golden Notebook* as young women in the 1960s and rereading the novel in middle age. Both recount dramatic first responses; McCrindle notes 'Then I thought it was the most courageous book I had ever read – both in its structure – keeping the different parts separate and connected in order to express and avoid chaos – and in its honesty of content.'[8] Elizabeth Wilson records her initial responses to Lessing and de Beauvoir: 'In the strange cultural landscape of 1960 they loomed up, Cassandras of women's experience, an experience that was everywhere silenced, concealed and denied.'[9] Yet both McCrindle and Wilson, as women involved with contemporary feminist movements, go on to record serious reservations about *The Golden Notebook*'s representation of twentieth-century woman. Wilson is especially critical of Anna Wulf's feeling 'bounded within masculine sexuality'. *The Golden Notebook* inspires very mixed readings.

Anna Wulf, the narrator–protagonist of the novel, is no Martha Quest waiting for a destiny. Initially Anna appears to be 'a free woman', a term she will use in the plural as the title of a novel. She is the author of a successful first novel, *Frontiers of War*, which gives her a measure of financial freedom. But that first success becomes an obstacle to Anna's continued work since so much of her energy is given over to subtle (and not so subtle) warfare with film producers who take options on her novel. The financial support provided by the novel and film options allows Anna who is nearing 40 to rear her daughter, do volunteer work for the Communist Party, and brood over the past. She also spends considerable time in analysis with Mother Sugar (Mrs Marks) who treats her for a growing ennui; Anna tells her analyst that ' "I've had experiences that should have touched me and they haven't" ' (GN, p. 232). The only writing she is able to do between the celebrity of her first book and the breaking of her writer's block is in the notebooks (black, red, yellow, blue) that form the bulk of the narrative in Lessing's novel. Dividing her life into her past experiences in Africa and their translation into her first novel, Anna constructs the black notebook. That notebook is followed by entries about her political life in the red notebook which is, in turn, followed by Anna's attempt to write a novel, *The Shadow of the Third*, about a character named Ella in the yellow notebook. Finally, Anna writes a blue notebook, a realistic record, she thinks, of daily events. The notebook entries (in order: black, red, yellow and blue) are divided by sections of a novel of manners entitled *Free Women*, the modest work focusing on Anna's relationship with her friend Molly and completed by Anna after she overcomes her writer's block, a searing process recorded in the single golden notebook.

The black, red, yellow, and blue notebooks testify to a terrifying personal and professional fragmentation 'as if Anna had, almost automatically, divided herself into four' (GN, p. 55). Divorced and responsible for a young daughter, Anna Wulf's life appears full of activity – social, political, and sexual. Those appearances, however, are deceptive; fragmentation plagues Anna as woman and as writer. She is overwhelmed by events, a situation captured in her obsessive collecting of newspaper head-lines: '[At this point the diary stopped, as a personal document. It continued in the form of newspaper cut-tings, carefully pasted in and dated]' (GN, p. 239).

Anna Wulf has become excessively subjective and separate from others. Responding to Mother Sugar who presses her to write again, Anna says, ' "Why can't you understand that . . . I can't pick up a newspaper without what's in it seeming so overwhelmingly terrible that nothing I could write would seem to have any point at all?" ' (GN, p. 251). She retreats into deeper and deeper silence. She has also developed some sense of superiority in connection with her ability (and inability) to write. She does not write because she cannot write the kind of book she admires: 'Yet I am incapable of writing the only kind of novel which interests me: a book powered with an intellectual or moral passion strong enough to create order, to create a new way of looking at life' (GN, p. 61). Not capable then of writing the masterwork, Anna is initially incapable of settling for less; she keeps her gift pure and criticises the lack of integrity in the movie people who try to adapt *Frontiers of War*.

In *Portraits of the Artist in Contemporary Fiction*, Lee T. Lemon argues that 'Anna struggles toward a new understanding, a less arrogant acceptance of what she is capable of doing.'[10] While much has been written about the formalistic experimentation in *The Golden Notebook* and about its daring topicality, Lemon's view rightly emphasizes the ethical – even Victorian – dimensions of the novel. The obvious fragmentation of form invites separating Lessing from the nineteenth-century masters she has claimed as literary ancestors, away from the traditional realism that she championed in the 1950s. Yet when examined closely the form of the novel yields a very tight structure, a control over fragmentation. At the same time, the traditional realism which Lessing praised was never monolithic for, as George Levine argues, realism has always been a complicated term: 'Whatever else it [realism] means, it always implies an attempt to use language to get beyond language, to discover some non-verbal truth out there.'[11]

For all of Anna's comments about fragmentation and dislocation, ultimately the novel acknowledges the need to pursue integration, wholeness. Lessing's novel does not finally inscribe a post-modern view as that view is described by N. Katherine Hayles: 'the realization that what has always been thought of as the essential, unvarying components of human experience are not natural facts but social constructions'.[12] In *The Golden Notebook*, Lessing presents sexual relationships as 'essential, unvarying com-

ponents of human experience'. Near the end of the novel,
Anna Wulf describes her strongest need as ' "being with
one man, love, all that. I've a real talent for it" ' (GN,
p. 625). Hayles rightly comments on 'The consistency with
which double standards for men and women appear in *The
Golden Notebook* and elsewhere in Lessing's writing . . .'[13]
Certainly Jenny Taylor speaks for many Lessing readers –
and critics – when she avers 'in the context of the
contemporary Women's Movement the novel certainly
isn't an explicitly feminist text'.[14]

Like Martha Quest, Anna Wulf often defines herself in
relationship with men. Whether waiting to cook for her
lover Michael who leaves her (blue notebook) or serving as
secretary to Communist organisers (red notebook) or
finding herself attracted to George Hounslow's masculi-
nity (black notebook) or describing her character/double,
Ella's, dependency on her lover Paul (yellow notebook) or
getting a first line of a novel from Saul Green (golden
notebook), Anna is, as Elizabeth Wilson noted, 'bounded
within masculine sexuality'. Anna worries about inviting
'defeat from men' and being 'stuck fast in an emotion
common to women of our time, that can turn them bitter,
or lesbian, or solitary' (GN, p. 480). Heterosexual relationships are central to *The Golden Notebook*.

Male empowerment is also crucial in Anna's creative life.
Above, I mentioned Saul Green's giving Anna the first line
of her second completed novel. Long before her involvement with Saul, however, Anna situates herself (as Lessing
had done in 'A Small Personal Voice') in relation to a male
creative pantheon. Noting that the function of the novel is
changing, Anna bemoans the absence of 'the quality a
novel should have to make it a novel – the quality of
philosophy' (GN, p. 61). Her touchstone is '. . . Thomas
Mann, the last of the writers in the old sense, who used the
novel for philosophical statements about life' (GN, p. 60).
Male, too, are the possessors of wisdom who watch Anna,

Saul, and other boulder-pushers work on the great black mountain of human stupidity: 'Meanwhile, at the top of the mountain stand a few great men' (GN, p. 628). Later when revisiting her past, imaged as films, Anna has her Virgil a projectionist, always identified as he, who selects the shots and goads her into recognition and responsibility: 'The projectionist now being silent, I called to him, "It's enough", and he didn't answer, so I leaned out my own hand to switch off the machine' (GN, p. 635). Anna needs her male masters.

Paradoxically, however, Anna's creativity and sexuality also support Elizabeth Hardwick's view of *The Golden Notebook*'s lasting significance for women. Lessing creates a portrait of an artist, not a portrait of the artist. Her artist figure is a woman and a woman with strong domestic and social ties. Anna Wulf is not separate from ordinary life; she is immersed in it. Eleven years after the publication of *The Golden Notebook*, Iris Murdoch published her portrait of an artist, and a blocked one at that, in *The Black Prince*; her artist figure is the male Bradley Pearson. And while there are a number of startling similarities between the two portraits, the gender difference in the artist figures makes a dramatic difference in the range of experience described.

That range of experience, and in particular sexual experience, also marks the importance of *The Golden Notebook* because as Rachel Brownstein observes 'it articulates certain facts that had previously been unmentionable'.[15] My agreement with Brownstein has to be explained with reference to Virginia Woolf. In Chapter 3, I referred to *A Proper Marriage* as the site of Lessing's killing of 'the Angel of the House'. I was then thinking of Woolf's talk to the Women's Service Society in 1921 when she described her origin as a writer and her contest with the Victorian stereotype 'the Angel of the House'. In that same talk, later printed as 'Professions for Women', Woolf went on to describe another obstacle:

I want you to imagine me writing a novel in a state of trance. I want you to figure to yourselves a girl sitting with a pen in her hand, which for minutes, and indeed for hours, she never dips into the ink pot. The image that comes to my mind when I think of this girl is the image of a fisherman lying sunk in dreams on the verge of a deep lake with a rod held out over the water. She was letting her imagination sweep unchecked round every rock and cranny of the world that lies submerged in the depths of our unconscious being. Now came the experience, the experience that I believe to be far commoner with women writers than with men. The line raced through the girl's fingers. Her imagination had rushed away. It had sought the pools, the depths, the dark places where the largest fish slumber. And then there was a smash. There was an explosion. There was foam and confusion. The imagination had dashed itself against something hard. The girl was roused from her dream. She was indeed in a state of the most acute and difficult distress. To speak without figure she had thought of something, something about the body, about the passions which it was unfitting for her as a woman to say. Men, her reason told her, would be shocked. The consciousness of what men will say of a woman who speaks the truth about her passions had roused her from her artist's state of unconsciousness. She could write no more.[16]

Elsewhere, I have called the obstacle Woolf could not overcome 'the Angel of the Body'.[17]

In *The Golden Notebook* Lessing kills 'the Angel of the Body' and gets close to what Woolf said she and no other woman writer had been able to do: 'telling the truth about my experiences as a body'. Lessing does this on the level of fiction and metafiction as Anna records her own physical experiences and as she analyses the problems of a woman writer writing about sex. In the yellow notebook Ella/ Anna/Lessing celebrate the vaginal over the clitoral orgasm, the emotional over the mechanical attitude toward sexuality:

> A vaginal orgasm is emotion and nothing else, felt as emotion and expressed in sensations that are indistinguishable from emotion. The vaginal orgasm is a dissolving in a vague, dark, generalised, sensation like being swirled in a warm whirlpool. There are several different sorts of clitoral orgasms, and they are more powerful (that is the male word) than the vaginal orgasm. There can be a thousand thrills, sensations, etc., but there is only one real female orgasm and that is when a man, from the whole of his need and desire, takes a woman and wants all her response.
>
> (GN, p. 216)

That celebration has caused all sorts of responses, positive and negative, responses which I want to avoid. Whatever the arguments about biology or sexual preference, the preceding quotation does put a woman's thinking explicitly about sexuality on a fictional map drawn by a woman. Later in the red notebook, Anna prepares for a day of political activity with a series of domestic chores which includes making the bed:

> As I pushed the stained sheet into the linen-basket I notice a stain of blood. But surely it's not time yet for my period? I hastily check dates, and realise yes, it's today. Suddenly I feel tired and irritable, because these feelings accompany my periods. (I wondered if it would be better not to choose today to write everything I felt; then decided to go ahead. It was not planned; I had forgotten about the period. I decided that the instinctive feeling of shame and modesty was dishonest: no emotion

for a writer.) I stuff my vagina with a tampon of cotton wool, and am already on my way downstairs, when I remember I've forgotten to take a supply of tampons with me.

(GN, p. 339)

Like Lawrence, Lessing sees sexuality as life-giving and she links Anna's healing to an erotic encounter that begins at a critical time in Anna's life.[18] Her daughter, Janet, leaves for a conventional boarding school, forcing Anna into a new role:

Coming back to the train, I thought again how strange it is – for twelve years, every minute of every day has been organised around Janet, my time-table has been her needs. And yet she goes to school, and that's that. I instantly revert to an Anna who never gave birth to Janet.

(GN, p. 577)

With Janet's departure, Anna plays a romantic and parental role to a younger lover, the American writer, Saul Green.

Anna's sexual involvement with Saul Green leads to her first direct acknowledgement '"that I have a writer's block"' (GN, p. 604). Yet involvement is an inadequate word to describe the weeks that Saul and Anna spend in her London flat. Through erotic energy, Anna finds herself. The weeks with Saul which begin with Anna's matter of fact recognition – 'It then occurred to me I was going to fall in love with Saul Green' (GN, p. 557) – are an ordeal in which Anna takes on Saul's madness. Anna's flat becomes both battleground and laboratory. Invaded by a myriad of personalities, Anna and Saul enact a variety of roles as both confront their pasts (Saul, too, is unable to write). A marathon of sex, anger, jealousy, and loneliness

gradually leads Anna from the fragmentation that occasioned the four notebooks to a moment when she decides
'I'll start a new notebook, all of myself in one book' (GN,
p. 607).

Challenging 'the Angel of the Body' so that Anna the
character's sexual experiences receive direct and due
attention is done at some cost for Anna the narrator
who must battle against 'the instinctive feeling of shame
and modesty' that prohibits explicitness about female
sexuality. For Lessing the problem is closer to being
solved than it was for Woolf but 'the Angel of the Body'
remains very much an adversary for a woman writer in the
second half of the twentieth century. Yet however traditional and romantic Anna's responses to sexuality (and
Lessing's as she suggests the power of nature – 'instinctive
feeling of shame and modesty') her very awareness as a
writer of the 'difficulty of writing about sex' (GN, p. 214)
and her courage in confronting that 'difficulty' continues
to make *The Golden Notebook* an important text for
women readers, whether they call themselves feminist or
not.

4 'Charting the New Territory': *The Four-Gated City*

If we are not channels for the future, and if this future is not to be better than we are, better than the present, then what are we?

(P8, p. 39)

After writing *The Golden Notebook*, Lessing returned to the completion of her long-planned *Children of Violence*, a return marked by a decided narrative emphasis on the future rather than the present or the past. Another title for *Landlocked*, the fourth volume in the series, might have been *Timelocked*, for everywhere there are signs that temporal as well as spatial constraints will have to be overcome by Martha Quest. The 'star's different time-scale' (L, p. 386) of which Thomas Stern speaks attracts Martha more than the quotidian chronology which regulates her activities in the colony as she awaits her chance to begin a life in England. Lorna Sage notes that *Landlocked* 'is haunted by an almost savage impatience for a different vision'.[1] Martha is much less drawn to the ordinary-time line of Johnny Lindsay's memoirs than to the complicated and mystifying interpenetration of past, present, and future in Thomas Stern's 'sheaf of stained damp papers' (L, p. 269), papers that she carries to England.

Actually from the beginning of the series, Lessing often positions Martha Quest toward a future time, a rather necessary device in a series which begins as a *Bildungsroman*. As Martha marries Douglas Knowell at the end of *Martha Quest*, Lessing stresses the temporality of the relationship; as she leaves marriage and motherhood at the close of *A Proper Marriage*, Lessing ironically underscores Martha's need for a vision of the future in her misunderstanding of Mr Maynard's question, ' "Well, what are you going to do now?" ' (p. 345). Even though 'overwhelmed with futility' (p. 262) in the last lines of *A Ripple from the Storm*, Martha begins to break away from Anton Hesse's intellectual aridity; the novel ends with Anton 'already freshly analyzing the situation' and Martha sliding 'into sleep like a diver weighted with lead' (p. 262). But in Lessing country sleep is the province of dreams with their potential for change. *Landlocked* itself closes with an opening as Martha and Jasmine Cohen prepare to leave Southern Rhodesia: Jasmine to Johannesburg and activity against the Nats, Martha to England and a much vaguer future.

The Four-Gated City opens after Martha's crossing of the geographical frontier; now living in England she is looking for an identity that will fit her new setting. In some ways, the Martha of the fifth volume of *Children of Violence* faces problems similar to those faced by the adolescent Matty in the first volume of the series. Once again, Martha Quest (now Hesse) is both alien and outsider, observing but not participating in communities. Whether in Stella's kitchen by the docks or with Iris and Jimmy in 'Joe's Fish and Chips', Martha suffers from a sense of dislocation, 'calling strange identities into being with a switch of clothes or a change of voice' (F-G, p. 17). Yet the narrative voice establishing an ironic distance from the protagonist in *Martha Quest* is not the narrative voice of *The Four-Gated City* where Martha Quest's point of view is emphasized – a change, I think, occasioned by Lessing's interest in crossing psychological as well as physical frontiers and the need to have a central consciousness in which to stage the crossing.

Martha's intense dislocation – at once estranging and empowering – is there from the first chapter of the novel where she goes in pursuit of the English in various locales. Unlike Doris Lessing who recorded a similar search in an earlier work, *In Pursuit of the English* (1960), Martha Quest does not find a matey atmosphere in a boarding-house. Rather she acts more as a secret agent watching fairly strange as well as common forms of life. She operates through a series of disguises as she interacts with working- and middle-class Londoners. Given the political passion in earlier volumes of *Children of Violence*, Martha might be expected to act as a more vigorous social critic than she does in *The Four-Gated City*. Observations about the resilience of the working class, the smugness of the middle class, and the omnipresence of the memory of the Second World War make up some of the narrative in Chapter One; far more interesting, however, are Martha's observations about her inner state.

Martha acts as cartographer and draws two very different maps.[2] One map captures the social life of London, its communities charted in terms of proximity to the Thames: 'For Martha, the river was still the point of reference in the chaos of London' (F-G, p. 13). The other map exists apart from spatial and social markers. On that map, Martha charts her inner state: 'She had learned that if she walked long enough, slept lightly enough to be conscious of her dreams, ate at random, was struck by new experiences throughout the day, then her whole self cleared, lightened, she became alive and light and aware' (F-G, p. 35). A 'whole self cleared', however, is but a first step to the centre of the second map; no Ayn Rand, Lessing does not endorse raw individualism, a self separate from other

selves in *The Four-Gated City*. Martha's journey is toward
the yearned-for community of like psyches, a journey
through numerous experiences and relationships that
promise, but do not provide, a way into that community.

With Jack, another emigré from Southern Africa,
Martha explores her sexuality (much like the Anna–Saul
sexual marathons in *The Golden Notebook*). In Jack's
strange house, a house like his life pulled back from war's
destruction, sexual experience overcomes Martha's feelings
of separateness, of dislocation:

> when the real high place of sex is reached, everything
> does move together, it is just that moment when every-
> thing does move together that makes the gears shift up.
> Yet people regarded sex as the drainer, the emptier,
> instead of the maker of energy. They did not know. But
> why was it that people didn't know? There was a
> knowledge that was no part of our culture, hinted at
> merely, you could come across references. Or you
> stumble on it.
>
> (F-G, p. 61)

That knowledge proves insufficient when Martha com-
pares Jack to Thomas Stern whom she took 'seriously' (F-
G, p. 64). Through sexual experience, she and Thomas
reached another level of knowing; for Jack, orgasm is the
final destination: 'With Jack, you set up a simple communion of the flesh, and then your mind went off by itself' (F-
G, p. 63).

In a very odd move much later in *The Four-Gated City*
Lessing converts Jack from the man who loved women
into a sexual predator stalking procurements for his
brothel. Jack's house which in Part One causes Martha
to feel 'instantly . . . at home' (F-G, p. 47) becomes in Part
Three 'an elaborate stage or setting for fantasies of
perverse sex' (F-G, p. 385). For Jack the experiences of

the body have become everything; for Martha Quest (and for Doris Lessing) the body is an instrument for transcendence, a transcendence made most dramatic in Martha's relationship with Lynda Coldridge.

Jack's house is an important station on Martha's journey, a marker on the psycho-spiritual map that comes to dominate Martha's enterprise. But that domination takes years, as another station, the Coldridge house on Radlett Street, proves a more permanent setting for the peripatetic Martha Hesse. She enters the house in Bloomsbury as a prospective employee. Brought to Mark Coldridge by his sister-in-law Phoebe, a political activist, Martha recognises the threat that the house represents:

> Standing in the hall of the house, which had Persian rugs on the dark floor, and a minimum of old furniture, Martha knew that for the first time in her life she was in a setting where if she chose to stay, there would be no doubt at all of how she ought to behave, to dress. She had always resisted such a setting, or the thought of it. If she took this job, then it must be for a very short time. She felt attacked by the house – claimed.
>
> (F-G, p. 85)

The claim is initially manifest as social with Martha acting as housekeeper–lover–secretary–editor for Mark Coldridge and surrogate mother for his son, Francis, and nephew, Paul, orphaned by his mother's suicide and father's defection to Russia.

On one level of the narrative, Lessing crosses the political novel with the novel of manners. Through Martha Quest's interaction with the extended Coldridge family over the years from the Cold War in the 1950s through Aldermaston in 1961 to a nuclear accident in the 1970s and its aftermath, Lessing maps the social, political, and cultural life of London. The Coldridge household weathers a number of what Mark Coldridge terms ' "tricky situations" ' (F-G, p. 89): among them, the fierce political battles between the Left and Right in the 1950s, the generational tensions between Mark and his son and nephew, the youth revolution of the 1960s, and psychological breakdowns in many of its inhabitants. And Martha, at or near the centre, knows the temptation of a public life – its demands and its celebrity.

On one level, *The Four-Gated City*, provides a public history of English society over three decades, offering what Jeannette King refers to as 'a solid and specific historical reality'.[3] Lessing's narrative energy and scope is reminiscent of George Eliot's to whom I compared her in Chapter 1. I fully agree with Gore Vidal who argues that 'Doris Lessing has more in common with George Eliot than she has with any contemporary serious-novelist'.[4] Earlier I focused on commonality of origins among authors. Here I want to explore common dissatisfactions with genre constraints: for Lessing in *The Four-Gated City*, for Eliot in *Daniel Deronda* (1876).

Both writers prize realistic social detail, a point that is essentially self-evident in the texts cited. Both writers ultimately emphasise the communal rather than the individual. As Gillian Beer notes: 'Instead of the desolate privacy of the Romantic ego, or the moral types of neo-classicism, George Eliot is seeking communal insights.'[5] So, too, Lessing opts for community over the individual in the final volume of *Children of Violence*, which begins by focusing on *Martha Quest* and ends by focusing on *The Four-Gated City*. For both writers, however, community comes to mean more than existing realistic protocols can contain.

The social realities in Eliot's London of the 1860s and Lessing's London of the 1950s and 1960s are finally not enough for either writer. In what Gordon Haight has termed 'her only novel of contemporary life',[6] Eliot faces an English society which is spent and imagines new beginnings in Kabalism. A century later, Lessing faces an English society that is spent and imagines new beginnings through Sufism. For both writers, the future of the many assumes a spiritual rather than a social or political cast, a cast that conventional realism cannot accommodate. Hence, in both *Daniel Deronda* and *The Four-Gated City*, Eliot and Lessing seek a hybrid form that could accommodate the spiritual – or to employ Eliot's pejorative word, the oracular, a term that Eliot used in an essay written long before *Daniel Deronda*.

Shortly before turning to the writing of fiction, George Eliot published 'Silly Novels by Lady Novelists' in the *Westminster Review* (October 1856). A number of interesting observations issue from that famous essay but none more fascinating than Eliot's condemnation of 'the *oracular* species – novels intended to expound the writer's religious, philosophical, or moral theories'.[7] Using a novel titled *The Enigma* as her example, Eliot goes on to decry that:

> confusion of purpose which is so characteristic of silly novels written by women. It is a story of quite modern drawing-room society – a society in which polkas are played and Puseyism discussed; yet we have characters and incidents, and traits of manner introduced which are mere shreds from the most heterogeneous romance.[8]

Twenty years after deriding silly women and their sillier novels for their 'confusion of purpose', George Eliot's last novel, *Daniel Deronda*, was being attacked by critics for its own 'confusion of purpose'. Similar critical disquiet has visited *The Four-Gated City*. Critical hostility, however, is not all that *Daniel Deronda* and *The Four-Gated City* have in common.

As George Levine has brilliantly argued in *The Realistic Imagination* George Eliot approaches the mystical (or that 'invisible world' that Eliot derided as the aim of oracular lady novelists) in *Daniel Deronda*. In twenty years of writing fiction Eliot moved her genre loyalty from a passionate adherence to a true picture of the visible world to an interpenetration of realistic and romantic modes, an interpenetration that intractable realists saw as a confusion of purpose or a lessening of her powers. In her career as novelist, Eliot moved from an adherence to the regularity of causal sequence toward the uncertainty in *Daniel Deronda*, a novel aptly described by Gillian Beer as 'haunted by the future'.[9] A similar movement is present in the career of Doris Lessing and most dramatically evident in *The Four-Gated City*.

Like Eliot, Lessing turned oracular and confounded many of her readers as she moved from emphasis on the discrete individual in a specified milieu to an emphasis on species. Ultimately in *The Four-Gated City* it is the second map that Martha charts, the map of inner states, of new ways of seeing and hearing, that dominates the narrative. The 'solid and specific historical reality' that Jeannette King sees Lessing presenting in much of *The Four-Gated City* proves a trap to Martha who through Lynda Coldridge's mentoring learns to prize the psychic instability that leads to resilience and the unexpected. With Lynda, Martha goes through an initiation at odds with solidity, with specificity:

> Martha descended night after night, when the day's business was over, to talk to Lynda, during that part of the day when they could be alone and undisturbed.
>
> They called it 'working'.
>
> But they did not know what to call it, nor how to go about it.
>
> Questions. It was a private, diffident pursuit of – but if they had known what to call it, then they would have known where to start. And they had to be secret – not

because of any decision made or taken, but because circumstances ordained it.

Mark could not be upset – Mark found it all very upsetting.

The children must not be diverted from their *proper* education, must not be allowed to feel any more unusual than they were bound to be anyway.

(F-G, pp. 354–5, italics mine)

Given the onus of 'proper' for Lessing, descent becomes the right way of learning and Lynda Coldridge the right teacher. Like Mordecai in *Daniel Deronda*, Lynda has psychic powers, which through much of her life has made her a victim of propriety. Released from one of her many incarcerations in mental institutions, Lynda returns to Radlett Street not to be claimed by the house and the power of the proper but to establish a different order in the basement. Initially, that order frightens Martha who sees Lynda's world 'as if it was a territory full of alien people from whom she had to protect herself, with whom she could have no connection' (F-G, p. 211).

Gradually, however, Martha's own experience of estrangement present from the beginning of the narrative – 'she would take a bus to Bayswater and spend the evening drifting in and out of the pubs with the other visitors, migrants, freebooters' (F-G, p. 20) – is transferred to the second and more important map in *The Four-Gated City*. The map, itself, undergoes changes and is no longer just a chart of an individual's inner state:

She thought, or wondered: is it in Lynda's head or in mine? And, with a shock of impatience against her own obtuseness (for surely she had been here often enough not to have to ask, or wonder): well, of course, it is not a question of 'Lynda's mind' or 'Martha's mind'; it is the human mind, or part of it, and Lynda, Martha can

choose to plug in or not. Which she had known, had
known well – this business of charting the new territory
meant a continual painful effort of discovery, of trying
to understand, to link, to make sense, and then falling
back again, 'forgetting': and then an effort forward
again – a baby trying to walk, that was what she was;
but surely there was no need for it, it was inefficient, for
obviously it was not possible that Lynda, Martha, were
the only two people who tried to make maps of these
territories. It must be a question of looking for, and
finding, the right guides.

(F-G, p. 473)

Like George Eliot, Lessing moves from an emphasis on the
destiny of the individual – an emphasis prescribed by the
Bildungsroman – to what Gillian Beer has described as a
'fascination with survival and development for the race,
the culture, and for mind'.[10]

The very structure of *The Four-Gated City* underscores
the movement from an emphasis on the fate of Martha
Quest, Mark, Coldridge, and a myriad of other individuals
to 'survival and development for the race, the culture, and
for an emphasis on the mind'. The four-part structure that
Lessing standardised for the first four volumes of *Children
of Violence* gets an 'Appendix' in *The Four-Gated City*. But
the conventional idea of 'appendix' as supplemental to the
book itself does not hold for the final volume of Lessing's
first series. Without the 'Appendix' *The Four-Gated City*
could be read as locked into Martha's fate as an individual,
with the protagonist musing about her solitude as a party
closes the formal novel. But Lessing is not writing *Mrs
Dalloway*, with its homogeneous idea of community; the
'here' that captures Peter Walsh's rapture at the end of
Woolf's novel is clearly attached to an individual. The
'here' of the last line in *The Four-Gated City* is attached to

a locale, what Lessing herself in later novels termed 'inner-space'.

A fuller and more comprehensive presentation of the implosion in the individual and the exploration of inner-space is the work of novels written after *The Four-Gated City*. In her conclusion to *Children of Violence*, Lessing must first explode maps of external space, hence, the 'Appendix' and its record of a world beyond London and English social history. One possible subtitle for the 'Appendix' is 'Apocalypse and After', recording as it does a dramatic change in existing political maps. After 'the Catastrophe' (F-G, p. 584), Britain is 'Destroyed Area II', implying other areas in a sequence of destruction. The progressive world has moved beyond Europe, but as in the four parts of the novel proper, there are two maps in the 'Appendix', one more consequential than another. Information about new political configurations, based principally in Africa and Asia, are provided by a variety of official documents and private letters.

That political map, however, is secondary to an evolutionary map, charted by the dying Martha Hesse, on Faris, an island off Scotland. Writing in 'an old school exercise book' (F-G, p. 596) and without benefit of political or social title, Martha records a new beginning: 'When we arrived we had half-a-dozen babies, infants, two of them without parents, a dozen growing children, half parentless, some young adults who soon coupled off, as well as the middle-aged or old' (F-G, p. 602). From this group a community emerges, a community based on 'our belief in a future for our race' (F-G, p. 604). Ultimately, such belief produces ' "The new children" ', seven children with advanced capacities; one of the seven is Joseph Batts, a child sent by Martha to Francis Coldridge, 'working as Deputy Head of the Reconstitution and Rehabilitation Area, near Nairobi' (F-G, p. 562). At the close of the

'Appendix', Joseph, 'classed 3/4 Negroid (on appearance)' (F-G, p. 609) and an alien, is cleared to learn gardening in his new environment. The 'marvellous child' (F-G, p. 609), as Martha describes Joseph Batts, is the channel for a future as yet unmarked on any political map.

5 Parables of Inner Space: *Briefing for a Descent into Hell, The Summer Before the Dark,* and *The Memoirs of a Survivor*

Our civilization represses not only 'the instincts', not only sexuality, but any form of transcendence. Among one-dimensional men, it is not surprising that someone with an insistent experience of other dimensions, that he cannot entirely deny or forget, will run the risk either of being destroyed by the others, or of betraying what he knows.

R. D. Laing[1]

Sufism is taught, not by tedious methods of 'A to Z' textbooks or teachings, but by the interplay of the minds of the teacher and the taught.

Insan-i-Kamil[2]

While R. D. Laing's statement underscores the thematic concerns of the three novels that Lessing published after completing *Children of Violence*, Insan-i-Kamil's description in 'The Sufi Path' might also be used to describe formal departures in those same novels. *Briefing for a*

Descent into Hell (1971), *The Summer Before the Dark*
(1973), and *The Memoirs of a Survivor* (1975), in varying
degrees, focus on characters at odds with their societies
because of 'experience of other dimensions'. The novels
present the conflicts between one- and multi-dimensional
people in narrative structures that undercut what many
might see as the 'tedious methods of "A to Z"' in the
traditional realist novel. The theme itself, particularly in
the examination of the meaning of normal, is not new to
Lessing. Indeed, *The Four-Gated City* maps Martha's
exploration of that terrain so much that Joan Didion
notes 'one would have thought Mrs Lessing had more or
less exhausted its possibilities'.[3]

What Lessing actually exhausts in *The Four-Gated City*
is a form that she herself identifies in the 'Author's Notes'
to that novel where she writes:

> This book is what the Germans call a *Bildungsroman*.
> We don't have a word for it. This kind of novel has been
> out of fashion for some time. This does not mean that
> there is anything wrong with this kind of novel.

But the novel preceding the note says something else.
The *Bildungsroman* with its emphasis on the development
of the individual ceased, even in *The Four-Gated City*, to be
a form that would accommodate changes in Lessing's view
of the relationship between the individual and the community. In Chapter 4, I observed that Lessing, like George
Eliot, moved her genre loyalty from realism to a hybrid
form which I termed the 'oracular'. That form allowed
Lessing to move her emphasis from the individual, what
Anna Wulf in *The Golden Notebook* terms 'the human
personality, that unique flame' (p. 71), to the species.

A movement from the one to the many of necessity
entails a change in the meaning of the term 'character'. The
conventional notion of character in the realist novel,

suggesting as it does singularity and separateness, does not serve Lessing's interest in more and more blurring – even eradicating – such distinctions in favour of a spiritual commonality. Like D. H. Lawrence, Lessing had come to question the importance given to 'the human personality, that unique flame'. In an oft-quoted letter to Edward Garnett, Lawrence disavows interest in:

> The old-fashioned human element – which causes one to conceive a character in a certain moral scheme and make him consistent. The certain moral scheme is what I object to. In Turgenev, and in Tolstoi, and in Dostoievsky, the moral scheme into which all the characters fit – and it is nearly the same scheme – is, whatever the extraordinariness of the characters themselves, dull, old, dead.

In sum, Lawrence's objections were much more radical than just opposition to 'the moral scheme into which all characters fit'. His very assault was on the conception of character itself. In place of the fixed and the final, 'the old stable *ego* of the character', Lawrence spoke for:

> another *ego* according to whose action the individual is unrecognisable, and passes through, as it were, allotropic states which it needs a deeper sense than any we have been used to exercise, to discover are states of the same single radically unchanged element. (Like as diamond and coal are the pure single element of carbon. The ordinary novel would trace the history of the diamond – but I say, Diamond, what! This is carbon! And my diamond might be coal or soot, and my theme is carbon.)[4]

Despite all of Doris Lessing's praise of Tolstoy, Dostoevsky and others who could write with authority

about the 'human element', praise that informs an early
essay like 'A Small Personal Voice' and the 'Preface' to
The Golden Notebook written about twenty years later,
Lessing had moved closer to Lawrence's concern with
'allotropic states' by the time she was writing *Briefing for
a Descent into Hell*. Lessing's nostalgia for the golden age
of the realist novel had given way to the creation of what
she termed in the Knopf edition of *Briefing for a Descent
into Hell* as 'Inner-Space Fiction – For there is never
anywhere to go but in'.

Briefing for a Descent into Hell opens with the problem
of identifying a patient admitted to the Central Intake
Hospital (institutional uniqueness is also blurred in this
narrative). Only the patient's sex – male – can be named
and nurse and doctor offer a few speculations about how
he got to the hospital and where he might have come from.
Soon enough, however, possible names are provided by the
patient in short dialogues with medical authorities inter-
spersed with first-person monologues to which presumably
only the reader is privy. In dialogues and monologues, the
patient is Charlie, or Jonah, or Jason, or Odysseus, or
Sinbad; he is, as Roberta Rubenstein maintains, 'Every-
man, rediscovering (remembering) through the exploration
of the microcosm of his own consciousness the experience
of the human race'.[5]

In the first part of the novel, the action prior to the
identification of the patient, Lessing's ultimate interest is
with the carbon, 'the pure single element' of which
Lawrence writes. The journey which Charlie relives in his
monologues takes him and the reader through a variety of
fantastic experiences quite at odds with the drab hospital
setting, itself very much an institutional inner space.
Carried by a friendly porpoise, Charlie escapes shipwreck
and comes to a land inhabited by friendly leopards, or
pumas, or 'whatever' (B, p. 38) who encourage him to
explore the vast terrain. Exploration leads to 'This city, or

town, or fortress' (B, p. 49), a locale of which Charlie becomes caretaker as he waits for the descent of the Crystal. The waiting period proves rife with dangers and temptations as strange women lure Charlie to bloody rituals and a population of rat-dogs and apes take over and despoil Charlie's city. The waiting period and its threatening events provide some of the most vivid and detailed writing in *Briefing for a Descent into Hell* as Lessing works toward the most important episode in the first part of the novel: Charlie's experience in the Crystal.

Charlie's absorption by the Crystal is Lessing's attempt at directly depicting the carbon, 'the same single radically unchanged element' in Lawrence's terms; the 'We' rather than the 'I' in Lessing's terms. First of all, Charlie is caught up in a lyrical and often overripe hymn to his experience of cosmic unity first imaged as 'a mosaic' reminding the reader of Yeats's attempt at rendering another experience of transcendence in 'Byzantium'. Then cosmic harmony is light but not light:

> In this great enclosing web of always-changing light, moved flames and tones and thrill of light that sang and sounded, on deeper and higher notes, so what I saw, or rather was part of, was neither light nor sound, but the place or area where these two identities become one.
>
> (B, pp. 97–8)

The preceding quotation captures the chief problem faced by Lessing in trying to shape Charlie's cosmic experience: Charlie as accounting for 'what I saw' versus Charlie as experiencing 'or rather was part of'. In electing to try to present the experience as ongoing, Lessing runs into the wall of words, the limitation of language. A far more effective attempt at presenting a direct experience of the carbon would wait for *The Making of the Representative for Planet 8* in 1982.

Because of his experience of cosmic harmony, Charlie
feels himself a messenger who must recount that experience
even through the inadequate medium of language. And
nowhere in the novel is Lessing's language more inadequate than in the embarrassing parody of conference
jargon she uses to translate Greek myth into 'the contemporary mode' (B, p. 123). At the conference on Venus,
Charlie is briefed (and not briefed) on the message of
harmony which he is to take back to an earth described as
'that Poisonous Hell' (B, p. 130). Shortly after receiving his
heavenly mission, Charlie the enlightened wakes up in the
Central Intake Hospital to find himself 'identified' as
Charles Watkins, Professor of Classics at Cambridge.

The Charles Watkins who emerges after being identified
through a family photograph is like and unlike Charlie the
visionary. Questioned and studied by doctors, Charles
clings to some of the details of Charlie's fabulous journey
and supplies a narrative of a wartime adventure in
Yugoslavia that appears to have been appropriated from
a friend. But that appropriation of Miles Bovey's experience among the partisans, rather than discrediting Charles
Watkins's veracity, acts as a link to Charlie and the
journey in inner space where any number of narratives
are appropriated by the voyager. Like the Robert Graves
of 'To Juan at the Winter Solstice', Lessing endorses the
view that 'There is one story and one story only'; the
emphasis again is on the carbon rather than the individual
ego, the unchanging rather than the unique.

The Charles Watkins who emerges from the letters of
wife, mistress, and colleague, however, seems as far away
from cosmic harmony as anyone can be, locked as he is in
smugness and selfishness. But another epistolary account
from a stranger, Rosemary Baines, presents a Charles
Watkins closer to the heavenly messenger. The variety of
accounts certainly subverts conventional chronology and
the reader's anticipation of moving from 'A to Z', but

Briefing for a Descent into Hell, like *Landlocked* and *The Four-Gated City* reflects Lessing's well-documented interest in Sufi thought. Even more, *Briefing for a Descent into Hell* reflects Sufi method, what 'The Sufi Path' describes as 'the interplay of the minds of the teacher and the taught'. Lessing seeks to structure a parable that will engage and challenge the reader.

Structure is the important word here since it suggests much more authorial control than 'interplay of the minds' does. It is a word that suggests more of the hierarchy and difference that informs even seemingly open-ended Sufism. For all of the suggestions in Sufi thought that the message of the parable has a life of its own, the messenger is still a figure of authority. There is, after all, a difference in levels of knowledge between the teachers and the taught. In her reading of *Briefing for a Descent into Hell*, Katherine Fishburn contends that Lessing is interested in the reader's involvement with a dialectic: Charlie's world in opposition to the doctors. Lessing, according to Fishburn, is interested in 'the process itself, our intellectual and imaginative engagement with the dialectic'.[6] That is interpreting the Sufi idea of 'interplay of the minds' without considering the mediation of narrative authority.

The opposition that Fishburn describes is carefully structured by Lessing in favour of Charlie the voyager rather than Charles the professor. In the first part of the novel, Lessing's strategy is to decrease emphasis on the activities at the Central Intake Hospital and increase emphasis on Charlie's direct experience of exhilaration. In Part Two, the letters presenting a negative view of Charles – from his wife Felicity, his colleague Jeremy, his mistress Constance – are effectively countered by one of the longest letters in the history of the novel, Rosemary Baines's letter to Charles, written after she has heard him lecture on the evils of standardised education. Baines, a retired headmistress, acts as a corroborater of Charles's function as messenger of cosmic harmony and reveals herself and others, especially Frederick Larson the archaeologist, as having a similar mission of remembering 'that something better than oneself is possible' (B, p. 162). Ultimately, Katherine Fishburn comes to the conclusion that product, the message or world view that Lessing proposes, is as important as process in the novel; Fishburn closes her reading by noting that Lessing 'challenges us to join Charles in his miraculous journey to points unknown. If we accept the challenge, we too will experience the awful joys and madness of transcendence. We too will dare disturb the universe.'[7]

In the end, however, transcendence proves short-lived for Charles Watkins who cannot remember. He loses his gamble that the shock treatment prescribed by the doctors will restore to him his 'real' memory, his memory of the message he is to bring to Earth. In R. D. Laing's terms Watkins has 'run the risk' and been destroyed by others. From the point of view of the establishment, represented by the doctors, the treatment works and his social role seems to be intact, for, as Jeremy Thorne, a colleague, writes: 'Felicity tells me you are restored to yourself. It goes without saying that I am delighted' (B, p. 275). Most readers will not be delighted with this triumph of 'normalcy' because, despite some ragged edges, particularly stylistic, *Briefing for a Descent into Hell* convincingly delivers what Betsy Draine calls 'a "Message" that is at once an admonition, a proposition about reality, and a way of seeing the world'.[8]

Lorna Sage has a different view of *Briefing for a Descent into Hell* and the novel that followed it, *The Summer Before the Dark*. According to Sage, 'both confirm the suspicion that, having turned her style and her way of thinking inside out, Lessing had for the moment depleted her resources as a writer. Whatever her convictions on the matter, the territory of speculative fiction was new to her;

and she explored it, to begin with, without subtlety.'[9] I think that Sage's judgement is closer to the mark for *The Summer Before the Dark*. In fact in that novel, 'the territory of speculative fiction', the world of inner space, is constantly threatened by the insistent sociological commentary of the omniscient narrator. One of the most successful counterweights against that threat in *Briefing for a Descent into Hell* is Lessing's manipulation of first- and third-person narration. Charlie's account of his journey in the first part of the novel establishes a necessary bond between cosmic messenger and sceptical reader, a bond which survives the unflattering first-person accounts of Watkins's wife and others. No such intimacy is constructed for narrator and reader in *The Summer Before the Dark* where inner and outer space are charted by an omniscient narrator.

While not sharing the narrative energy of *Briefing for a Descent into Hell*, *The Summer Before the Dark* does share some of the same thematic concerns. In both novels the phenomena of constructed appearance, especially of socially constructed appearance, threaten inner space. Both novels locate much of that threat in the official language used to label and, therefore, contain or limit 'reality'. Charlie's experiences in the Central Intake Hospital question the conventional meaning of normalcy, sleep and light, among other terms. Kate Brown's life 'among words, and people bred to use and be used by words' (SD, p. 244) spurs her to take a non-verbal stand by not dyeing her hair.

Like Charles Watkins, Kate Brown at 45 is middle-aged and in crisis: 'With not so much as a room of her own' (SD, p. 19). Her crisis, however, has more sociological than cosmic implications. No longer needed by her family and exiled from her home which her husband has let for the summer, Kate Brown is forced into 'private stock-taking' (SD, p. 5) and into recognising that her unease is very much related to her gender-role, her role of wife and mother:

The small chill wind was blowing very definitely, if still softly enough: this was the first time in her life that she was not wanted. She was unnecessary. That this time in her life was approaching she had of course known very well for years. She had even made plans for it; she would study this, travel there, take up this or that type of welfare work. It is not possible, after all, to be a woman with any sort of mind, and not know that in middle age, in the full flood of one's capacities and energies, one is bound to become that well-documented and much-studied phenomenon, the woman with grown-up children and not enough to do, whose energies must be switched from the said children to less vulnerable targets, for everybody's sake, her own as well as theirs. So there was nothing surprising about what was happening. Perhaps she ought to have expected it sooner?

(SD, p. 19)

Too often, however, the omniscient narrator presents Kate neither as the individual character of realist fiction nor the everywoman of a parable but as a specimen of 'a well-documented and much-studied phenomenon'.

The tension throughout the novel is between Kate's exploration of inner-space and the literal journey she makes from England, to Turkey with Global Food, to Spain with a younger lover, back to London where she shares a flat with a younger woman, and then to home. Lessing uses Kate's memories of a privileged girlhood spent in England and Africa as well as her memories of her marriage to map deftly the social constructs which shape the life of a middle-class woman. Much of the terrain has been travelled by Martha Quest, particularly in *Martha Quest* and in *The Four-Gated City*, but in those novels the protagonist worked through anger and rage toward another definition of self. Kate Brown is no Martha Quest. Moving between past and present, Kate is able to understand if not destroy (a lack that has not endeared the novel to some feminist readers) the stereotypes that have defined her role as wife and mother. There is a good deal of anger not fully acknowledged by either character or narrator in the memories that fuel part of Kate's inner life. A sequential dream about a seal, a device that becomes too predictable and even prosaic, makes up the rest of Kate's inner life. Indeed, the best part of the dream sequence is what it reveals about Lessing rather than what it reveals about Kate Brown.

Kate's first experience of the dream is described as 'like the start of an epic, simple and direct' (SD, p. 29). *The Summer Before the Dark*, in fact, reveals Lessing's appropriation of devices from the masculine epic form; there are indications of this in the novel's opening *in medias res*, the appropriation of the journey motif, the allusions to the arming of the hero in the passages about Kate's clothes and hairstyles, the episodic presentation of the journey as Kate faces a variety of tests from which she emerges in triumph of a scaled-down sort:

Her experiences of the last months, her discoveries, her self-definition; what she hoped were now strengths were now concentrated here – that she would walk into her home with her hair undressed, with her hair tied straight back for utility; rough and streaky, and the widening grey band showing like a statement of intent.

(SD, p. 244)

The traditional epic form had been used to validate a particular social order; Lessing upends that genre expectation and converts her epic devices into social criticism. But an epic, whether praising or criticising, requires the presentation of a society, an outer space which Lessing provides in Kate's experiences first as a translator for Global Foods, then as a runaway to Spain, and finally as an exile in London. In all of the novel's locales, Lessing offers trenchant social commentary of world organisations, the travel patterns of the young, the sexism of British workmen, and the like. The problem for the reader is that both inner and outer space are recorded by the same omniscient narrator whose magisterial voice is more appropriate to the analysis of societal stereotypes faced by women than to the protagonist's inner explorations presented most directly in the sequential dream of taking a seal back to the ocean. Lessing's difficulty in *The Summer Before the Dark* is an omniscient narration that is more attuned to outer than to inner space.

No such problem exists in *The Memoirs of a Survivor* where, as Ruth Whittaker observes, 'For the first time in Doris Lessing's work, realism and symbolism mesh totally.'[10] Much of that success lies in Lessing's use of first-person narration for her parable of destruction and creation. *The Memoirs of a Survivor* is narrated by an unidentified older woman, who, like Kate Brown in *The Summer Before the Dark*, is engaged in 'stock-taking'. Unlike the stock-taking in the preceding novel, however, stock-taking in *The Memoirs of a Survivor* is both private and public as the narrator acts as memoirist not just for herself but for the 'we' to whom constant appeal is made.

The intimacy missing from the narration in *The Summer Before the Dark* is present in the relationship between narrator and reader in *The Memoirs of a Survivor*; so, too, is the full authority missing from Charlie's account in *Briefing for a Descent into Hell*. There Charlie's narration is challenged by third-person accounts in the exchanges of the doctors and the first-person accounts in letters from wife, mistress, and colleague. No authorial challenge is levelled at the narrator of *The Memoirs of a Survivor* who from time to time astutely questions the accuracy of her own remembering:

> Is it possible that this is the stuff of real memory? Nostalgia – no, I'm not talking of that, the craving, the regret – not that poisoned itch. Nor is it a question of the importance each one of us tries to add to our not very significant pasts: 'I was there, you know. I saw that'.
>
> (M, p. 4)

The effect works so that the reader grows more trusting of the tale – and what a tale. What the survivor–narrator describes is the death of modern civilisation as experienced in a large, unnamed city.

Lessing had toured the country of apocalypse before, in the 'Afterword' to *The Four-Gated City*, but that novel quickly fled urban life in London in favour of Martha's island and other outlying settlements. No such ordinary flight would any longer satisfy Lessing who had moved farther away from political topography; the solution would have to come through inner space. The outer space of *The Memoirs of a Survivor* is at first a city where civil authority has broken down. The remaining middle class, given its language by a powerful and ubiquitous broadcasting network, go on pretending that things are normal. Soon enough, though, things change as citizens leave the city and other groups described as gangs and tribes take over for indeterminate periods of time. More and more, the urbanscape is closer to the world of Auden's 'The Shield of Achilles'. What the narrator survives is a dystopian world familiar enough from George Orwell and Anthony Burgess. How the narrator survives is distinctly Lessing.

The narrator lives alone in a block of flats originally built with private money for the middle class, but homogeneity has disappeared from the migratory world of *The Memoirs of a Survivor*. As the narrator explains:

> What it amounted to was that a flat, a house, belonged to the people who had the enterprise to move in to it. So, in the corridors and halls of the building I lived in, you could meet, as in the street or a market, every sort of person.
>
> (M, p. 6)

Initially, however, the narrator, ever the polite neighbour, is less involved with the outer world:

> and all this time my ordinary life was the foreground, the lit area – if I can put it like that – of a mystery that was taking place, had been going on for a long time, 'somewhere else'. I was feeling more and more that my ordinary daytime life was irrelevant.
>
> (M, p. 11)

The narrator becomes more and more absorbed by her own inner space which Lessing craftily presents as the inner space of the flat – the world behind the living-room wall. Soon that absorption, that focusing leads to the narrator's being able to go 'through the wall' and recognise that 'this place held what I needed, knew was there, had been waiting for – oh, yes all my life. I knew this place, recognised it' (M, p. 13). But realisation and acceptance of the possibility of going through the wall are but the beginning of a learning process for the narrator, retold in anything but the 'tedious methods of "A to Z"' as a teaching story for the reader. What Lessing seeks to do in *The Memoirs of a Survivor* is to construct a parable of inner space that takes the reader through the process of the narrator's becoming what Katherine Fishburn has termed 'the guide-leader or mediator'.[11] No such process is made clear in *Briefing for a Descent into Hell* and the limited process that is presented in *The Summer Before the Dark* is too personalised in Kate Brown to have the larger applicability that Lessing is after in *The Memoirs of a Survivor*.

Lessing, after all, is not wedded to a rugged individualism that stresses a unique history; the narrator of *The Memoirs of a Survivor* speaks for a 'we' not an 'I'. The Sufi concerns that inform the novel are what Lessing terms a 'combination of the mystic and the practical' (SPV, p. 133). Sufism is not a way of escaping outer space but a way of setting up the right order between inner and outer space. For Lessing, Sufism 'is not contemptuous of the world. "Be in the world, but not of it", is the aim' (SPV, p. 133). In a brilliant narrative strategy, Lessing keeps her narrator in the crumbling world of the novel through her relationship with Emily Cartwright, a girl of about 12 who is mysteriously left in the narrator's flat. At some point after her first experience in the world through the wall the narrator records: 'the child was left with me in this way. I was in the kitchen, and, hearing a sound, went into the living-room, and saw a man and a half-grown girl standing there' (M, pp. 14–15). Earlier the narrator noted 'That the wall had become to me – but how can I put it? I was going to say, an obsession' (M, p. 11). No such single focus is possible once the narrator is given the responsibility of Emily and Hugo, the child's cat-dog.

At the outset, that responsibility seems to thwart the narrator's journey within:

And this is my difficulty in describing that time: looking back, it is as if two ways of life, two worlds, lay side by side and closely connected. But then, one life excluded the other, and I did not expect the two worlds ever to link up. I had not thought at all of their being able to do so, and I would have said this was not possible.

Particularly now, when Emily was there; particularly
when I had so many problems that centred on her being
with me.

                                                    (M, p. 25)

Linkage, of course, is the very point of the parable, but for
purposes of discussion, I will temporarily unlink the two
worlds and turn to the relationship between older woman
and younger girl, a relationship less effectively examined in
The Summer Before the Dark, and the 'many problems that
centred on her being with me'.

The problems associated with Emily exist on both sides
of the wall. In the outer space, the narrator participates in
the rapid changes in her society as Emily moves from
young child protected in the narrator's flat to young
woman seeking the communal life outside. The narrator
and Hugo are left waiting and watching as Emily becomes
part of Gerald's gang, an ever-changing collection of
younger and younger children who create an extended
family and an economy based on barter and theft. The
domestic order created by Gerald and Emily as surrogate
parents to the younger, ever-more-violent children, like
other forms of order gives way to greater social chaos
which invades even the narrator's building as its top floors
become the haven of savage children. No longer the
admired leader, the Pied Piper, Gerald joins Emily,
Hugo, and the narrator 'waiting for winter to end' (M,
p. 215).

The world of action represented by Gerald's attempt to
craft a new social order in his house gives way to the
narrator's flat whose space has become a staging area for
another life. Emily's adventures in the outer world
watched by or recounted to the narrator have been
paralleled by the activities through the wall. Even in that
world Emily plays a part as the narrator experiences two
different settings:

One, the 'personal', was instantly to be recognised by the air that was its prison, by the emotions that were its creatures. The impersonal scenes might bring discouragement or problems that had to be solved – like the rehabilitation of walls or furniture, cleaning, putting order into chaos – but in that realm there was a lightness, a freedom, a feeling of possibility. Yes, that was it, the space and the knowledge of the possibility of alternative action. One could refuse to clean that room, clear that patch of earth; one could walk into another room altogether, choose another scene. But to enter the 'personal' was to enter a prison, where nothing could happen but what one saw happening, where the air was tight and limited, and above all where time was a strict unalterable law and long – oh, my God, it went on, and on and on, minute by decreed minute, with no escape but the slow wearing away of one after another.

(M, pp. 41–2)

At various stages in her life through the wall, the narrator enters the 'personal' scenes that explain not just Emily's but also her own social conditioning in the traditional family which like the traditional society in *Memoirs* has come to a dead end. Coming to understand what has led to Emily's difficulties, the narrator comes to understand her own past: ' "It starts when you are born", I said "It's a trap and we are all in it" ' (M, p. 132).

The way out of the trap of the personal is provided by the discipline of the other realm behind the wall. The narrator is changed by her experiences of creation and destruction in the impersonal world through the wall:

A restlessness, a hunger that had been with me all my life, that had always been accompanied by a rage of protest (but against what?) was being assuaged. I found that I was more often simply waiting. I watched to see

what would happen next. I observed. I looked at every
new event quietly, to see if I could understand it.

(M, p. 102)

That change empowers the narrator, finally, to lead others
from the collapsing 'real' world through the wall at the end
of the novel. In a scene where as Lorna Sage notes 'the
novel crumples up its world like a sheet of paper',[12]
Lessing attempts to frame a transcendent experience and
once again, as in *Briefing for a Descent into Hell*, runs into
the limitation of language. Trying to describe 'the one
person I had been looking for all this time' the numinous
being who leads the group 'into another order of world
altogether', the narrator finally concludes 'all I can say is
. . . nothing at all' (M, pp. 216–17). What Lessing is canny
enough to do in *The Memoirs of a Survivor* that she could
not do in *Briefing for a Descent into Hell* is reach that
mystical silence before straining after the poetic rapture
that encumbers the earlier novel.

6 'Many a Planet by Many a Sun': *Canopus in Argos*

Every night my father took out his chair to watch the sky and the mountains, smoking, silent, a thin shabby fly-away figure under the stars. 'Makes you think – there are so many worlds up there, wouldn't really matter if we did blow ourselves up – plenty more where we came from'.

Doris Lessing (SPV, p. 93)

'Cast a cold eye
On life, on death.
Horseman, pass by!'

W. B. Yeats[1]

About mid-way in *The Memoirs of a Survivor*, the narrator speculates that

all this time human beings have been watched by creatures whose perceptions and understanding have been so far in advance of anything we have been able to accept, because of our vanity, that we would be appalled if we were able to know, would be humiliated (p. 82).

Shikasta (1979), the novel that follows *Memoirs*, offers human readers plenty of opportunities to overcome vanity and to feel humiliation in the face of superior beings. In the

first volume of her second series, *Canopus in Argos*,
Lessing moves into outer space 'as a fully paid-up
alien',[2] and views Earth's history from the beginning of
humanity through the twentieth century. In 'Some Remarks' attached to *Shikasta*, Lessing celebrates the liberat-
ing experience of writing what she terms 'space fiction':

> It was clear I had made – or found – a new world for
> myself, a realm where the petty fates of planets, let alone
> individuals, are only aspects of cosmic evolution ex-
> pressed in the rivalries and interactions of great galactic
> Empires: Canopus, Sirius, and their enemy, the Empire
> Puttiora, with its criminal planet Shammat.
>
>   (S, ix)

As a reader situated in the 'old world' vacated by
Lessing, I find less to celebrate in *Shikasta* and two of
the novels that follow it: *The Sirian Experiments* (1980)
and *The Sentimental Agents* (1983). Awash in the ordinary
and less attracted to the long view, I agree with Nicole
Ward Jouve who argues:

> I'm not convinced that the way to trans-individuality is
> in disregard of, or contempt for, individuality, rather
> than *through* individuality. That the fate of Mary Turner
> is not more 'universally' relevant *because* so narrow and
> precise in its unfolding than the fate of the late Martha,
> or the various people who flit across SH [*Shikasta*] and
> can be catalogued as number 3 or number 8 terrorist.[3]

What Lessing seems to be continuing in *Canopus in
Argos* is her love–hate relationship (or guilt about) the
personal or the subjective or the individual. As early as
1957 Lessing wrote of the dangers of two positions: 'One
sees man as the isolated individual unable to communicate,
helpless and solitary; the other as collective man with a

collective conscience. Somewhere between these two, I believe, is a resting-point, a place of decision, hard to reach and precariously balanced' (SPV, p. 12). Fourteen years later in her 'Preface' to *The Golden Notebook*, Lessing described not a balance, 'a resting-point' between the individual and the collective, but a movement away from the individual toward the group:

At last I understood that the way over, or through this dilemma, the unease of writing about 'petty personal problems' was to recognise that nothing is personal, in the sense that it is uniquely one's own. Writing about oneself, one is writing about others, since your problems, pains, pleasures, emotions – and your extraordinary and remarkable ideas – can't be yours alone. The way to deal with the problem of 'subjectivity', that shocking business of being preoccupied with the tiny individual who is at the same time caught up in such an explosion of terrible and marvellous possibilities, is to see him as a microcosm and in this way to break through the personal, the subjective, making the personal general as indeed life always does . . .

(GN, xiii)

Seven years after writing her 'Preface,' Lessing distanced her interest in 'the tiny individual' even more dramatically in *Shikasta* where the term 'individual' seems an afterthought, coming in third behind 'cosmic evolution' and 'the petty fates of planets'. Now more concerned with the 'explosion of terrible and marvellous possibilities', Lessing casts a very cold eye 'On life, on death' in *Canopus in Argos*.

One means of distancing her narrative from 'the tiny individual' is her use of an archival structure for the series whose full title is *Canopus in Argos: Archives*. She had experimented with this format earlier in *The Golden Note-*

book, in the 'Appendix' to *The Four-Gated City*, and in *Briefing for a Descent into Hell*. The archival format is used most extensively in *Shikasta*, *The Sirian Experiments*, and *The Sentimental Agents*, where documents, reports and extracts proliferate and provide interminable details about the 'great galactic empires' that intrigue Lessing. In those same novels, distance is also increased by the presence of galactic administrators as central narrators. Johor, the Canopean agent in *Shikasta*, Ambien II in *The Sirian Experiments* (after her conversion to the Canopean way), and Klorathy, the Canopean agent in *The Sentimental Agents*, maintain the long view. Ruth Whittaker's judgement of the narrative in *Shikasta* applies as well to the other two novels: 'In *Shikasta* there is pain and difficulty for the narrator, but it is understood in the contexts of the cosmic scheme, and therefore the personal signifies little.'[4] The understanding described by Whittaker is something I want to connect to the site of the paternal in *Canopus in Argos*.

In Chapter 1, I discussed Lessing's emphasis on the father in her speculation about the shaping of a woman writer. The mother is connected with 'practicality, the ordinary sense, cleverness, and worldly ambition'; the father is weighted with 'dreams and ideas and imaginings'. Time and again in Lessing's first novel-series, *Children of Violence*, the father's ability to distance himself from the demands of ordinary life is pitted against (and often endorsed over) the mother's immersion in daily life. In Lessing's second novel-series, the war between father and mother continues, this time on a cosmic stage. Lessing dedicates *Shikasta* to her father in an abridged form of the section of 'My Father' which I quote at the beginning of this chapter. And the presence of the father's long view of our petty world accounts for much of the coolness or unemotional acceptance of what Claire Sprague terms 'the determinism that hangs so heavily over the Canopean cosmos'.[5] In an interview, Lessing chides Christopher Bigsby about his use of the term determinism: 'You keep talking about determinism. It is the opposite that I have experienced.'[6]

At the heart of *Canopus in Argos* is a colonial system much more evolved, much more complicated, and much more sanitised than anything Lessing wrote about in *Children of Violence*. In the earlier series, Lessing through her characterisation of Martha Quest positioned herself as a critic of the social, sexual, and racial hierarchies resulting from the British presence in Africa. *Canopus in Argos* has no central character as its focus, although Johor and Klorathy play prominent roles in at least four of the novels. But lack of central character does not preclude a central view from emerging, a view endorsing rather than rejecting hierarchies – at least the right hierarchies.[7] Right means Canopean. According to Lorna Sage, 'Her Canopeans are the ideal colonists, who rule by virtue of their more intimate understanding of the patterns of creation and destruction at work in the universe.'[8] Clearly, Lessing does not celebrate the economic guile and use of force that characterises the power attained by a Cecil Rhodes, but she does celebrate the power, benign of course, that Canopus exercises.

Canopean power is centred in its ability to feed SOWF ('the substance-of-we-feeling') to other planets. For the Canopeans, the species rather than the individual matters; for as Johor notes: 'To identify with ourselves as individuals – this is the very essence of the Degenerative Disease, and every one of us in the Canopean Empire is taught to value ourselves only insofar as we are in harmony with the plan, the phases of our evolution' (S, p. 38). The Canopeans seem to be the evolutionary outcome of the marvellous children the dying Martha Quest describes to Francis Coldridge: 'They all carry with them a gentle strong authority. They don't have to be shielded from the knowl-

edge of what the human race is in this century – they know
it . . . They include us in a comprehension we can't begin
to imagine' (F-G, p.608).

Gentle or no, the Canopeans exercise power over other
planets through SOWF and by their sending agents
throughout the galaxy. At every stage of Shikasta's
history, for example, Canopean agents appear in a variety
of guises to try to elevate the inhabitants of the wounded
planet (too little SOWF).[9] The same is true of other planets
in the galaxy; Canopean agents, whom Lorna Sage has
likened to wandering Sufi teachers bringing the word to
the uninitiated, are everywhere a little like the many British
teachers exported to colonial school systems. I do not
mean to suggest, however, that Lessing's Canopeans are
perfect. They, too, are subject to 'the Purpose, the Law, the
Alignments' (SA, p. 159). But since whoever or whatever
designed 'the Purpose' never appears in Canopus in Argos,
the Canopeans must be seen at the top of the world that
Lessing establishes in her colonisation of the galaxy. In
The Making of the Representative for Planet 8, for instance,
the narrator recognises the Canopean emissaries by 'an
authority they all had', but goes on to claim that authority
'was an expression of inner qualities, and not of a position
in a hierarchy' (P8, p. 3). Whatever the structure is called,
the Canopeans are at its peak.

Interesting as Canopean colonisation is, particularly in
Shikasta and sections of The Sirian Experiments, the
process itself becomes too episodic for a reader like myself
suffering from 'the Degenerative Disease'. Fortunately
Lessing takes some pity on 'our sad muddled minds' (S,
p. 364) and includes The Marriages Between Zones Three,
Four, and Five (1980) and The Making of the Representative for Planet 8 (1982) as volumes two and four in the
series. With very good reason, Betsy Draine labels the
books, sister volumes.[10] In both novels the settings are
more limited in scope, and the narratives are focused on

central characters (I hesitate to say individuals). Indeed personal problems seem less petty in the sister volumes of *Canopus in Argos* where microcosm as microcosm has its worth even apart from its service to the macrocosm.

According to Lessing, *The Marriages Between Zones Three, Four, and Five* 'has turned out to be a fable, or myth. Also, oddly enough, to be more realistic [than *Shikasta*]' (S, ix). What intrigues Lessing elsewhere in the series, 'the rivalries and interactions of great galactic Empires', give way to an older interest: the war between the sexes and its effects on individuals and societies. The locales in the three zones may be remote from the topography of Rhodesia and London, but the examination of gender roles is a familiar exercise in Lessing's fiction. Once again, as in the first three volumes of *Children of Violence*, marriage and its consequences are central to the novel.

Al·Ith, queen of Zone Three, and Ben Ata, king of Zone Four, are ordered by the 'Providers' (MBZ, p. 4) to marry and must acquiesce. (Presumably the Providers are Canopeans or even higher on the galactic chain, but Lessing's attention is elsewhere in this novel.) Much of the narrative is devoted to the sexual involvement between the rulers of the different zones and the personal and social implications of that involvement. From the beginning, the reader favours Zone Three over Zone Four because the narrator is Lusik, one of Zone Three's Chroniclers and one of Al·Ith's Mind-Fathers.

Unlike the administrators who narrate other volumes in the series, Lusik, like Doeg in *The Making of the Representative for Planet 8*, has a vested interest in the fate of the society and the individuals being described. As Katherine Fishburn notes:

Although he [Lusik] serves in an official capacity as chronicler, he does not enjoy the immortal status of

Johor or the other Canopean emissaries. What he writes, therefore, is not informed by any kind of galactic intelligence or perspective. All interpretations are his own and limited to his personal capabilities as an artist.[11]

Doeg, even more dramatically, is subject to mortality. In both novels, Lusik and Doeg are insiders in the narrative worlds they shape. Lusik's tale begins by emphasising 'our own harmonies, the wealths and pleasures of our land' (MBZ, pp. 5–6). Zone Three, as Marsha Rowe has observed:

> is a pastoral Utopia. It represents what Zone Four might become, if the creativity lodged in human labour were to be released by a transformation of the relations of production and reproduction, if 'feminine' values like responsiveness and nurturing were released through the entire social texture. Zone Three has no exploitation or oppression, no hierarchy based on force, privilege, or possession. Childcare is shared between the sexes and between biological parents and others. There is no sexual ownership – sexual monogamy is only ever temporary, and while a special value is attributed to nurturing the soul from the moment of conception onwards (in this idealised world no abortions are needed since conception only ever occurs by choice), a woman will conjoin with other men during pregnancy, men whose vibrations she feels are right for her and the child-to-be.[12]

Yet Zone Three is not without its problems. Like the militaristic Zone Four, it has become too self-contained and in its own pacific way, too regulated. Presumably, the Providers recognise a need to stir things up a bit by ordering Al·Ith to journey to Zone Four and wed its warrior king. In some ways the novel might be subtitled *Pride and Prejudice* with Al·Ith and Ben Ata smug about the social structures which each heads and contemptuous of other ways of living. Gradually, however, each is changed by experience of the other, experience which the tale delineates in a manner that Nicole Ward Jouve would term as 'narrow and precise in its unfolding' because of Lusik's focus on Al·Ith. Both rulers become exiles from their former selves, but it is Al·Ith's exile that most interests Lusik. Al·Ith's emotional and psychological changes are the heart of the tale. Her scepticism about the order from the Providers, her patience in teaching Ben Ata to reflect, her exasperation with the birth ritual in Zone Four, her curiosity with the blue of Zone Two, and her wail of loss when the Providers order her to separate from Ben Ata and their son are bold threads in Lusik's narrative, a narrative as much concerned with Al·Ith as individual as it is with Al·Ith as ruler of Zone Three.

Indeed it is Al·Ith as individual who brings Zone Two into the narrative. After her separation from her life with Ben Ata in Zone Four, Al·Ith returns to Zone Three to find herself replaced as queen by her sister: 'And soon Murti had to leave for her duties – Al·Ith's old duties. And Al·Ith knew that she was not going to be asked to take them over again, nor even share them' (MBZ, p. 190). Exiled from her past in Zone Three, and her present in Zone Four, Al·Ith turns toward a new duty, a future in Zone Two. The spiritual turning, however, is not without cost for Al·Ith whom Betsy Draine terms 'the unwilling pilgrim from one spiritual state to another'.[13] Even as she moves toward the frontier of Zone Two, Al·Ith is not without longing for her life with Ben Ata who, in response to the Providers, has wed Vashi, warrior queen of Zone Five. But move she does into the mystery of Zone Two.

As befits a novel in Lessing's galactic series, Lusik closes the tale with a description of collective rather than individual change:

> There was a continuous movement now, from Zone Five [Ben Ata has married its amazon queen] to Zone Four. And from Zone Four to Zone Three – and from us, up the pass [toward Zone Two]. There was a lightness, a freshness, and an enquiry and a remaking and an inspiration where there had been only stagnation. And closed frontiers.
>
> (MB, pp. 244–5)

Yet in depicting progress in the social structure, Lusik has not ignored the cost to the individuals who make up that structure. In *Marriages Between Zones Three, Four, and Five* what Nicole Ward Jouve terms trans-individuality does, in fact, come through rather than in disregard of individuality. With its attention to individual and society, Lusik's narrative comes close to the 'resting-point' which Lessing champions in 'The Small Personal Voice'.

The 'resting-point' in *The Making of the Representative for Planet 8* seems to many readers to be closer to a total acceptance of the collective. Jeannette King, for example, argues that Planet 8 'is a society, moreover, in which individualism as we know it is non-existent: the individual's role in society as a whole is what matters as it was in Rohanda's Golden Time'.[14] Certainly Planet 8 is a society structured around communal activities: adults are identified according to their work and the society is governed by fifty representatives of whom Doeg, the narrator/protagonist is one. Communal accord had long been the tradition on Planet 8:

> Usually it was evident what had to be done by everyone. We had never had to make speeches, or exhort, or

persuade, or demand – as I have seen done on other
planets, and read about. No, there had always been a
consensus, an understanding among us all, and this had
meant that it had been a question of: so-and-so will see
to this, and such and such will be done – by someone.
And it was at these times that a Representative who felt
a change was needed would step back into the mass, or
someone who felt entitled and equipped would step up
into the Representative group.

(P8, p. 75)

Much is shared by the citizens of Planet 8 who, according
to Claire Sprague, 'have already travelled far toward we-
ness when we meet them'.[15] But to argue for a communal
social order, like the one that exists on Planet 8, is not to
argue against the existence of the individual or, more
exactly, the person as the basis of that order.

Unquestionably, individualism as a political philosophy
is alien to the world view of Doeg and the other inhabitants of Planet 8. Individualism has always been an alien
political philosophy to Doris Lessing and her fiction; the
individual, however, is not an alien on Planet 8 or in other
worlds shaped by Lessing. Doeg, for example, writes of
'every individual in the land' (P8, p. 19); he notes that 'this
business of calamity . . . affects people so variously and
insidiously' (P8, p. 38). The calamity is first a change of
climate as Planet 8 moves from being a ripe and easeful
world to a place of ice. One of the effects of the climactic
change is a changing perception of individuality:

We would sit pressed together, as soon as the light went,
in some place where the snowdrifts were not so deep,
with our backs to the great barrier, and we ate our
tasteless and disagreeable dried meat, or roots of the
half-frozen rushes: and we dozed there as if we were one
organism, not many – as if our separate unique indi-

viduralities had become another burden that had to be
shed, like unnecessary movement.

(P8, p. 45)

Yet even as the calamity becomes more dire, Doeg
continues to record memories, a central element of personal and cultural identity.

What is happening on Planet 8 is nothing less than the
end of that world; Johor, the Canopean emissary, first
orders a wall built against the change in climate, a change
that threatens the planet with ice. Initially the wall works
and the citizenry is buoyed by the Canopean promise of an
airlift to Rohanda. Soon enough the wall begins to give
way and the promise of one kind of survival fades:
Canopus cannot fully control SOWF and, as a result,
Rohanda has become Shikasta – no place for the people
of Planet 8. Johor returns to participate in the last days of
Doeg's world, and like the true Canopean, he teaches a
lesson in obedience to the Necessity – in this case an
acceptance of the end. Claire Sprague likens *The Making
of the Representative for Planet 8* to 'Job's struggle to
understand apparently arbitrary affliction'.[16] In Lessing's
fable, Doeg the narrator is Job while Johor is a divine
messenger responding to human doubts and distress. Once
again, I find myself preferring Doeg's doubt and distress to
Johor's message.

Doeg is caught between a desire for signs 'that we had a
future. Our planet had a future' (P8, p. 9) and growing
'feelings of loss, even of anguish' (P8, p. 28) about the fate
of Planet 8. Even the presence of Johor and his message
about another order of being cannot fully extinguish
Doeg's yearning for the world of the past nor fully quiet
his/her (except among the young, gender is not specified in
the novel) 'cycle of pleas and of plaints, of grief – of
sorrowing rebellion' (P8, p. 80). Betsy Draine maintains

that 'Through Doeg, the reader is made to confront the pathetic and tragic aspects of "the grand plan" of evolution.'[17] But Doeg's questioning has no real chance against Canopean teaching and Johor's mission.

Simply put, Johor must make the surviving citizenry accept their physical death and the ice age that is overtaking their planet, an acceptance that involves the recognition of the constancy of change and the relativity of all things. Near the end of the tale, as the survivors of Planet 8 are journeying toward the pole to die, Doeg records the acceptance of the Canopean message:

> But the little dazzle or dance we looked at, the fabric of the atomic structure, dissolved as we watched: yes, we saw how those old bodies of ours inside their loads of hide were losing their shapes, how the atoms and the molecules were losing their associations with each other, and were melding with the substance of the mountain. Yes, what we were seeing now with our new eyes was that all the planet had become a fine frail web or lattice, with the spaces held there between the patterns of the atoms.
>
> (P8, p. 118)

Obviously, Doeg's recognition here and elsewhere on the trek to the pole signifies the triumph of the Canopean long view. Yet it is a triumph that is forced and at times muddled because even as Doeg seems to be celebrating the one, 'a fine frail web or lattice', awareness of individuality is still very much evident:

> The Representative swept on and up, like a shoal of fishes or a flock of birds; one, but a conglomerate of individuals – each with its little thoughts and feelings, but these shared with the others, tides of thought, of

feeling, moving in and out and around, making the
several one.

(P8, p. 119)

Katherine Fishburn observes 'that even as part of the
Representative, Doeg retains at the very least a memory
of himself as an individual – albeit an individual who, with
the slightest variation, could have been someone else'.[18]

In *The Making of the Representative for Planet 8*, Doris
Lessing offers her most sustained and effective presentation of an evolutionary collective and still cannot abandon
the individual. Amidst 'the rivalries and interactions of
great galactic empires', Lessing may find the fate of the
individual petty but nonetheless compelling.

7 Re-entry: *The Diaries of Jane Somers, The Good Terrorist,* and *The Fifth Child*

They cannot scare me with their empty spaces
Between stars – on stars where no human race is.
I have it in me so much nearer home
To scare myself with my own desert places.

Robert Frost[1]

Looking over the literary terrain in Britain in the mid-1950s, Doris Lessing declared: 'We are not producing masterpieces, but large numbers of small, quite lively, intelligent novels. Above all, current British literature is provincial' (SPV, p. 15). That declaration was made as Lessing was in the middle of writing *Children of Violence*, a series that could be labelled neither small nor provincial. Twenty-three years later, Doris Lessing spoke with Christopher Bigsby and declared:

> The five-volume or three-volume realistic novel seems to me dead, the family novel. Well, maybe it is not dead, but I am not interested in it. I am much more interested in a bad novel that doesn't work but has got ideas or new things in it than I am to read again the perfect small

novel. I read somewhere the other day that in 1912 in China when the civil war was all around they were still writing the most exquisite little poems about apple blossom and so on, and I have nothing against exquisite little poems about apple blossom and I very much enjoy reading the small novel about emotions in the shires, but I do regard it as dead.[2]

That declaration was made as Lessing was in the middle of writing *Canopus in Argos*, a series filled with 'ideas or new things' and situated far from the shires.

Those observations about novels, dead and alive, point to an anxiety about performance in the Lessing who has so often praised novels of ideas written by men. It is an anxiety she herself explores in *The Golden Notebook* as Anna Wulf grapples with her desire to write a big novel, like the novels written by her male literary heroes: 'a book powered with an intellectual or moral passion strong enough to create order, to create a new way of looking at life' (GN, p. 61). If 'Free Women' is the evidence Anna Wulf never writes that novel, but, as Lee Lemon has observed, Doris Lessing does write that novel and publishes it as *The Golden Notebook*.

What I want to stress here is the ongoing tension in Lessing between the values of the big novel which she associates with ideas, experimentation, and usually male authors, and the small novel which she associates with emotions and convention. I want also to link that tension to Lessing's description of the 'creation of a woman novelist' in her essay on Olive Schreiner. There she writes of 'a balance between father and mother' (SPV, p. 108) as an essential ingredient. But the 'resting-point' between paternal and maternal influences (the mother's practicality offset by the father's dreaming) has been as difficult to reach as the 'resting-point' between the many and the one in Lessing's work. Judith Kegan Gardiner observes:

Early in her career, Lessing defined her esthetic choices in gendered terms, her 'feminine' and implicitly 'masculine' short stories marking out different ways of approaching history and working over complementary psychological issues. In the 1980s, forty years after her first stories, her aesthetic choices of space fiction and romantic novels seem equally gender-polarised. However, her extraordinary productivity in the intervening period has not proceeded along neatly divided lines; rather, these polarising tendencies in her work involve enormously fruitful and continuous renegotiations of insoluble contradictions.[3]

I would not go so far as Judith Gardiner to argue that *Canopus in Argos*, which she terms 'space fiction', and *The Diaries of Jane Somers* (1983), which she reads as a romantic novel, are 'gender-polarised'. In all her novels, Lessing constantly tries to negotiate a balance between paternal and maternal influences, trying to reach a psychic 'resting-point'. As indicated in Chapter 6, I do not see a balance between patriarchal and matriarchal values in *Canopus in Argos* which I would describe as gender-ascendant with the father's long view dominating; still the practicality and ordinary concerns that Lessing long associates with the mother find their place in *The Marriages Between Zones Three, Four, and Five* and in *The Making of the Representative for Planet 8*. In the three novels that follow the galactic series, *The Diaries of Jane Somers*, *The Good Terrorist* (1985), and *The Fifth Child* (1988) maternal concerns are ascendant. All three novels explore relationships in unconventional families, especially mother–child relationships; all three novels examine issues of generational as well as societal responsibility. In *The Diaries of Jane Somers*, *The Good Terrorist*, and *The Fifth Child*, Lessing re-enters earth's atmosphere and breathes new life into what she terms 'the family novel', a form she had pronounced dead in her interview with Christopher Bigsby.

Before *The Diaries of Jane Somers* was published by Doris Lessing in 1984, the two narratives that make up the volume were published by Jane Somers: *The Diary of a Good Neighbour* in 1983 and *If the Old Could* . . . in 1984. Much has been made of Lessing's hoax and I want to make a bit more of the author's prank in Chapter 8. Here, though, I want to look at *The Diary of a Good Neighbour*, the most interesting and successful of the two narratives. In her first-person account, Jane Somers, who prefers to call herself Janna, offers a more mundane version of memoirs of a survivor; she is 'A handsome, middle-aged widow with a very good job in the magazine world' (DJS, p. 9). Alone after the illnesses and deaths of her husband and her mother, Janna thinks that 'I had let Freddie down and had let my mother down' (DJS, p.11) and feels some need to expiate by responding to an advertisement for friends for old people. But neither philanthropy nor the proximity of an older neighbour affect Janna Somers who has buried herself in her work as editor of *Lillith*, a contemporary women's magazine.

It is through her work that Janna Somers is able to see and become interested in the aged Maudie Fowler. Working on a feature article, 'Stereotypes of Women', Janna comes upon the sketch of a witch which she discards; the image, however, stays with her and causes her to notice Maudie Fowler in the chemist's: 'A tiny bent-over woman, with a nose nearly meeting her chin, in black heavy dusty clothes, and something not far off a bonnet' (DJS, p. 12). That connection springing from curiosity becomes, a bit too predictably, Janna's way out of emotional isolation as she becomes involved in Maudie's life and death. Claire Sprague has observed that 'Janna does change, but her changes are not dramatic. One could be cruel and say that instead of long soaks in her tub, she takes shorter ones and sometimes even skips a soak altogether'.[4] One reading of *The Diary of a Good Neighbour* might endorse the view that Lessing continues to see the fate of individuals as petty with her focus on Janna's bathing, her wardrobe, and her involvement in office politics. But that reading would have to ignore the complex mother–daughter relationship that evolves between Janna and Maudie who play both roles to one another. More importantly, so dismissive a reading would have to ignore Lessing's compelling presentation of ageing and dying in the narrative.

Ruth Whittaker aptly invokes Muriel Spark's name when she writes about *The Diary of a Good Neighbour*: 'With the exception of Muriel Spark, there are few contemporary writers who have dealt so powerfully with the taboo topic of growing old.'[5] Spark's economy of style in *Memento Mori* produces the telling detail as she meditates on the evil and good in the last days of a small group of friends and acquaintances. Always less economical as well as less wry than Spark, Lessing is more scatological than eschatological in her presentation of Maudie Fowler's world. It is a world of incontinency, grime, and smell; a world where more and more the body betrays any hope of going on and do-gooders threaten remaining dignity. It is also a world of pleasure in thoughts of the past, in tastes of real cream, in pride of independence. Long before Virginia Woolf wrote of it, Maudie had learned the value of a room of one's own: ' "That's the main thing", she [Maudie] said, "Training. It stands between you and nothing. That, and a place of your own" ' (DJS, p.19). In Maudie Fowler, Lessing creates an individual with a rich memory and whether or not it is 'lying nostalgia', Maudie's remembrance of the terrors and the delights of growing up in Victorian England anchors the narrative. Betrayed by her family, exploited by employers, and isolated by ageing, Maudie Fowler could have been robbed of her final dignity by Lessing and presented as a victim. But she is not, because of Lessing's careful and loving attention to her past and to her emotional complexity. Without that attention, the old woman would have been a case study instead of a character and Lessing would have been one of the faceless officials Maudie had come to see as a threat because they would treat her as a statistic rather than a person.

Which brings me to another of the strengths of *The Diary of a Good Neighbour*: Lessing's crafting of a human face for social services. From Maudie's point of view the Good Neighbours, Home Help, Meals on Wheels and other social agencies 'get up to anything' (DJS, p. 17), but Maudie's judgement is more the product of paranoia produced by loneliness than actual evidence. What Lessing offers is a picture of social agencies that are inadequate to the complexity and scope of the problems to be faced; she does not offer a picture of villains plotting against their clients. Indeed, Vera Rogers, the social worker who visits the old women in Maudie's building, works to better their lot, recognising the crippling limitations of what she can do. She, too, 'had to go home to her family problems' (DJS, p. 146). One of Janna's imaginative exercises is 'A Day in the Life of a Home Help' with its picture of Bridget whose sensitivity, good humour, and affection informs her work with demanding and forgetful old people. Bridget, too, has a home life filled with family demands. Finally, there are the nurses in the Old Hospital where Maudie lingers for several weeks before she dies; made up of the many races of twentieth-century Britain, they care for old women who often see them as aliens.

Of course most of the human faces attached to the various social services in *The Diary of a Good Neighbour* are women's faces. Care-taking, whether in the family or in the society, remains very much a gendered work even near the close of the twentieth century. Because she has a writer's curiosity and the time provided by widowhood and a well-paying occupation, Janna Somers chooses to follow Maudie out of the chemist's shop, to become entangled in her life. But for other women in Janna's narrative, care-taking is not so freely chosen and one measure of Janna's changed view of her world is her ability to see these women. Moving from *Lillith*'s complicity in stereotyping women as forever young or middle-aged, Janna comes upon Maudie Fowler and the world of ageing women whose existence makes jobs for a Home Help: 'She may be Irish, West Indian, English – any nationality, but she is unqualified and has a dependent of some kind or children, so that she needs a job she can fit around her family' (DJS, p. 181). Finally, flush with the success of her romantic novel, *The Milliners of Marylebone*, based on Maudie's life, Janna discovers new material in the ward maids:

> I want to write about these ward maids, the Spanish or the Portuguese or Jamaican or Vietnamese girls who work for such long hours, and who earn so very little, and who keep families, bring up children, and send money home to relatives in South-east Asia or some little village in the Algarve or the heart of Spain. These women are taken for granted. The porters are paid well in comparison; they go about the hospital with the confidence that goes with, I would say, not being tired. I know one thing, these women are tired.
>
> (DJS, p. 240)

Janna also recognises that her absorption in the lives of the ward maids 'is a possible new novel; but this time not a romantic one' (DJS, p. 240). Like Lessing, Janna Somers needs a realistic form for a different kind of family novel.

The Good Terrorist is another version of the family novel. Once again, London is the setting, and once again, the family at the centre of the narrative is a creation of adoption rather than generation. 36-year-old, university-educated, and unemployed, Alice Mellings is the good terrorist who tries to make a home for herself and her revolutionary companions in a London squat. Alice and her friends are the extreme representatives of a view Lessing described in 'Laboratories of Social Change', the last of the Massey Lectures she delivered on CBC in 1985. After applauding the triumph of democracy in Greece, Portugal and other countries, Lessing went on to note:

> In the balance against this hopeful fact, we must put a sad one, which is that large numbers of young people, when they reach the age of political activity, adopt a stance or an attitude that is very much part of our times. It is that democracy is only a cheat and a sham, only the mask for exploitation, and that they will have none of it. We have almost reached a point where if one values democracy, one is denounced as a reactionary. I think that this will be one of the attitudes that will be found most fascinating to historians of the future. For one thing, the young people who cultivate this attitude towards democracy are usually those who have never experienced its opposite: people who've lived under tyranny value democracy.
>
> (P, p. 64)

Alice, Jasper (her companion of fifteen years), Pat, Bert, Faye, Roberta, and the other comrades in the Communist Centre Union Squat not only believe that 'democracy is only a cheat and a sham', but they talk endlessly about its failures. As Ruth Whittaker observes 'Rhetoric is one of Mrs Lessing's principal satiric targets in this novel.'[6] The male comrades, in particular, are given to the exchange of slogans and abstractions, political language that has grown more hollow for Lessing since her earlier depiction of the private life of activists in the Mashopi sequences in *The*

Golden Notebook. In that novel, Anna Wulf recognises the pretence underlying the rhetorical pontification of Willi Rodde and Paul Blackenhurst, but Anna's recognition is wry rather than fierce, the only word to describe the narrator's response to the mechanical mutterings of Bert and Jasper. Number 43 is filled with rhetoric that inflates the fantasies of its inhabitants who finally blunder into action.

Alice Mellings is at the centre of Lessing's exploration of domestic terrorism. Using a third-person narrator as her agent, Lessing explores the contradictory impulses in Alice Mellings that led to her becoming the terrorist next door. The novel opens with Alice gazing at the squat she and Jasper are about to approach; her first comment displays some knowledge of buildings: ' "I should think 1910", said Alice. "Look how thick the walls are" ' (GT, p. 3). The novel closes with Alice, alone 'in the silent house. In the *betrayed house*' (GT, p. 450). Alice sits in the kitchen, clutching a mug of tea and 'looking this morning like a 9-year-old girl who has had, perhaps, a bad dream . . .' (GT, p. 456). Between opening and closing, Alice moves from some control over her life, typified in her interest in things outside herself like the dating of the building, to a reversion to childhood security when waking banishes the frightening images of night. What happens between those two views of Alice in *The Good Terrorist*, however, may have its origins in a bad dream or fantasy of revolutionary activity but it has its ends in a real home-made bomb that explodes and kills passers-by and terrorists alike.

The freedom of a third-person narration allows Lessing to offer ironic commentary on the action in and out of the squat; at the same time, by focusing on the consciousness of Alice Mellors, Lessing is able to centre a novel whose subject matter might tempt her to display what Betsy Draine brilliantly terms 'a conscience that wants to have its say in essay form'.[7] Lessing's choice of shaping the narrative around Alice Mellings checks any impulse to sermons that would diffuse narrative control. Choosing a woman terrorist as her focus also allows Lessing to return to a longstanding interest: the relationship between mothers and daughters. Allison Lurie and other reviewers have compared *The Good Terrorist* and Conrad's *The Secret Agent* (1907) as definitive representations of terrorist psychology, a comparison with which I agree. Even more interesting, however, is both Conrad's and Lessing's concentration on maternal energy in their accounts of the domestic lives of terrorists. In an 'Author's Note' written thirteen years after the publication of *The Secret Agent*, Conrad describes his shaping of the narrative:

> Slowly the dawning conviction of Mrs Verloc's maternal passion grew up like a flame between me and that background [the enormity of London], tingeing it with its secret ardour and receiving from it in exchange some of its own sombre colouring. At last the story of Winnie Verloc stood out complete from the days of her childhood to the end, unproportioned as yet, with everything still on the first plan, as it were; but ready to be dealt with.[8]

The story of Alice Mellings's 'maternal passion' gives Lessing the structure for *The Good Terrorist*.

Before becoming the good terrorist, Alice Mellings spent years as the good daughter in the prosperous middle-class home of her parents, Cedric and Dorothy Mellings: 'There had seemed to be a shine or gloss on Cedric and Dorothy, an aura or atmosphere about them, of success, of confidence' (GT, p. 247). But divorce and changed economic standards (Cedric has two families to support) disrupt the golden age that Alice remembers and she begins her political activity as much as a search for family as for social change. In a series of communal arrangements that begin while she is at university, Alice Mellings becomes the good mother:

> In the house in Manchester she had shared with four other students she had been housemother, doing the cooking and shopping, housekeeping. She loved it. She got an adequate degree, but did not even try to get a job. She was still in the house when the next batch of students arrived, and she stayed to look after them.
>
> (GT, p. 16)

She appropriates the maternal role which she saw her mother, Dorothy, play in the golden days of the Mellings; part of that role-playing involves Alice's frequent wearing of her mother's clothes. Alice, in turn, is appropriated by Jasper in a non-sexual relationship (he is homosexual) in which she can play parent and fantasise about playing wife. As one character in the novel observes, Alice is a prime case of arrested development.

Jeannette King links Alice Mellings with Mary Turner of *The Grass Is Singing*; King sees each woman split between two warring selves and ultimately incapable of healing that psychic division. That seems to me a fruitful comparison which I would like to address. Like the Mary Turner who at 30 is a successful secretary, Alice Mellings appears to be in control of her life. It is she who can negotiate with the housing authority and the police; it is she who can bring some order to the squat at Number 43, making it habitable for her comrades. That external control, however, is constantly threatened by her memories of her parents and the past and the 'lying nostalgia' of herself as the good daughter because the memories so often turn to rage and anger. Indeed Alice's most effective terrorist activities are carried out against her parents. She vandalises her father's property and steals his money. But her most intense love–hate relationship is with Dorothy

Mellings whom she exploits and idolises. Dorothy finally
breaks away from the relationship by selling the family
home, a move made necessary by the divorce and subse-
quent years of having Alice and Jasper live with her.
Dorothy Mellings has to run away from her daughter to
be free of terror; as Claire Sprague notes, 'The daughter
cannot escape her dependence, but the mother can. Dorothy abandons Alice instead of vice-versa.'[9]

Like Mary Turner whose memories of her parents'
sexuality inhibit her relationship with her husband, Alice
Mellings never reaches sexual maturity; hence her willingness to be exploited by Jasper. Like Mary Turner, Alice
Mellings has been educated beyond her mother's level; yet
neither Mary Turner nor Alice Mellings learns to think, to
analyse her situation. On one level, each is apparently able
and organised, Mary Turner as secretary and Alice Mellings as housekeeper; on another, the emotional level, each
is crippled by past experiences that she cannot understand
and move beyond.

Lessing's most dramatic presentation of the divisions in
Alice Mellings is in the novel's final scene. Alone in
Number 43 with no comrades to mother, Alice reverts to
the role of child: 'she felt that she could pull the walls of
this house, her house, around her like a blanket, where she
could snuggle, where she could feel safe' (GT, p. 451). Her
desire for security comes after participating in the bombing
of a hotel with material supplied by the IRA; one terrorist
has been blown up and all the others, save for Alice, have
departed. Alice's only companion is her fantasy life which
exonerates her of all responsibility: 'Not that Alice be-
lieved that she – Alice – had any real reason to feel bad; she
hadn't *really* been part of it [the bombing]. Alice sighed, a
long shuddery breath, like a small child' (GT, p. 451). But
even Alice cannot find haven in her fantasies about a
golden childhood, fantasies that centre on being her
mother's good girl: 'But today her mind would not stay

in this dream, or story; it insisted on coming back to the present, away from her mother, who was finally repudiating Alice because of the bombing' (GT, p. 454). The bombing has changed everything and, ironically, occasioned some recognition in Alice, but the final irony is that Alice's recognition has come too late. About to meet the mysterious Peter Cecil whom she thinks is 'MI6 or MI5 or XYZ or one of those bloody things, it didn't matter' (GT, p. 453), Alice is first confident that she can organise and handle things, a confidence totally undercut by the narrator's final image of her as 'the poor baby . . . waiting for it to be time to go out and meet the professionals' (GT, p. 456). Lessing closes *The Good Terrorist* with a bang and a whimper.

Domestic terrorism continues to engage Lessing in *The Fifth Child* where Ben, the title character, disrupts the near-perfect Lovatt family. The disruption, however, is unaccompanied by the political rhetoric and posturing so central to *The Good Terrorist*. Ben, in fact, has very little access to language; he is, as his mother Harriet notes at his birth, a 'poor little beast' (FC, p. 49) dramatically out of place in the Edenic world the Lovatts had been shaping for themselves. That shaping begins at an office party in 1960s London; described by the omniscient narrator as 'two eccentrics' (FC, p. 6), Harriet and David immediately recognise each other as outsiders in their freewheeling society. In what becomes the novel's chief irony, with the arrival of Ben Harriet and David see one another as throwbacks to earlier, happier social eras. Instantly, they fall in love, marry, buy a large suburban house and begin their perfect family.

For a time their script produces just what they want: precious children, family parties at holidays, and smugness. 'Listening to the laughter, the voices, the talk, the sounds of children playing, Harriet and David in their bedroom, or perhaps descending from the landing, would reach for each other's hand and smile, and breathe happiness' (FC, p. 18). David and Harriet cast themselves in starring roles in their production of the perfect family; '*We* are the centre of this family' (FC, p. 27) David tells his critical mother. But centres need supports, and Harriet and David exploit others to stage their extravaganza. Dorothy, Harriet's mother, is cast in the role of housekeeper: 'for, if family was what they had chosen, then it followed that Dorothy should come indefinitely to help Harriet, while insisting that she had a life of her own to which she must return' (FC, p. 14). David's father, James, is given the work of producer in the family saga and assumes the Lovatts' 30-year mortgage. Other relatives play smaller roles in the Lovatt family narrative; no part exists for Ben, their fifth child.

For one thing, Ben is not like Luke, Helen, Jane, and Paul, his siblings. Harriet recognises Ben's difference during her pregnancy and resorts to drugs:

> If a dose of some sedative kept the enemy – so she now thought of this savage thing inside her – quiet for an hour, then she made the most of the time, and slept, grabbing sleep to her, holding it, drinking it, before she leaped out of bed as it woke with a heave and a stretch that made her feel sick.
>
> (FC, pp. 40–1)

'It' survives pre-natal combat and becomes Ben, 'Eleven pounds of him. The others had not been more than seven pounds. He was muscular, yellowish, long. It seemed as if he were trying to stand up, pushing his feet into her side' (FC, p. 48). In a 1989 interview, Lessing describes Ben as one of 'the little people' (not as imagined by Disney Studios): 'I think that they were more likely to be like Ben – not exquisite fairies or charming little pixies or interesting gnomes, but creatures having to survive at all

costs, before fire, and probably living in caves or mountains.'[10] Ben brings his instincts of survival into the middle
of the Lovatt family and the terrorism begins. Killing a
dog, attacking his brother, stalking a thrush, Ben, as
Harriet notes '*is* absolutely *not* ordinary' (FC, p. 51).

Initially on the other side, Harriet finds herself support-
ing Ben in her own fight for survival. After bearing four
children, Harriet moves outside the greeting-card landscape, 'this miraculous kingdom of everyday life' (FC,
p. 61) she and David inhabited, into the imperfect real
world. Her exile from Eden produces an analytic complexity more and more highlighted by a third person narration
that delineates the changes in Harriet. First, she feels guilt
as life alters dramatically in the magic house: 'She knew
when they had seen him, because of the way they looked at
her afterwards. As if I were a criminal! she raged to herself'
(FC, p. 60). Then she starts questioning the evasive
language used by family and medical experts to contain
Ben. To David, 'He's a funny little chap' (FC, p. 48); to
Doctor Brett, Ben is a 'Naughty baby' (FC, p. 54); to his
brother Luke 'he isn't really one of us' (FC, p. 76). But
verbal containment proves insufficient in dealing with
Ben's difference, and finally the extended family decides
to institutionalise Ben.

Resistant to the decision, Harriet is helpless in the face
of family unity. That helplessness, however, is soon over-
powered by 'guilt and horror that kept her awake through
the nights' (FC, p. 77). Throughout her career, Lessing has
been intensely sceptical of institutional solutions to human
problems, particularly problems of dealing with difference.
Images of Lynda Coldridge facing the psychological
establishment in *The Four-Gated City* or the neat solutions found by the unnamed doctors in *Briefing for a
Descent Into Hell* come immediately to mind. But in those
novels and others, Lessing's scepticism is less directed
toward asking questions than in directing the reader to

the right answer. The medical establishment is no less a target (along with the school system) in *The Fifth Child*; Harriet correctly concludes that 'Everyone in authority had *not* been seeing Ben ever since he was born' (FC, p. 131). But social authority is less of an overpowering presence in the spare narrative than in previous novels. In *The Fifth Child* Lessing seems more intent on questioning than answering as she examines the family, the site of origin, and its capacity to cope with difference. As she told Hans-Peter Rodenberg in an interview:

> Well, what interests me most of all is that at the moment when the mother has to decide whether she's going to leave the child in the institution where he'll die, or take him home, that is absolutely the *heart* of our civilization, because we are committed *not* to killing the people born damaged or mental defectives or anything. This is our civilization and what we stand by. So there's no way that, *officially*, Ben could have been got rid of.[11]

The maternal choice becomes the universal in *The Fifth Child*.

Spurred by guilt, Harriet Lovatt drives 'to a place in the North of England' (FC, p. 78) to free Ben. What she discovers is a holding facility for children dumped by their families. No doctors are present, ' "Dr MacPherson isn't here this week" ' (FC, p. 79); only a tired young girl and a 'young man, in a white coat that was not clean' (FC, p. 80) are there to represent authority. (Here, as in *The Diary of a Good Neighbour*, Lessing underscores the failure of institutional solutions without savaging the human beings who do the daily work of institutions.) Harriet walks through a 'nightmare ward' : 'Rows of freaks, nearly all asleep, and all silent. They were literally drugged out of their minds' (FC, p. 81). In a separate room, Harriet finds a drugged Ben, straitjacketed and lying in excrement:

She did not know what to say. Her heart was hurting as it would for one of her own, real children, for Ben looked more ordinary than she had ever seen him, with those hard cold alien eyes of his closed. Pathetic: she had never seen him as pathetic before.

(FC, p. 83)

Momentarily overcome by 'maternal passion', Harriet takes Ben home, making a decision that leads to the end of the 'miraculous kingdom' she and David tried to create. In relation to 'maternal passion', I want to stress 'momentarily' because Harriet's chief connection with Ben is through maternal responsibility rather than 'maternal passion'. Ben seems almost human after the 'monsters' (FC, p. 81); he seems 'one of her own, real children'. But those feelings cannot last with Ben out of the straitjacket and back among her 'real children' who see her as choosing 'to go off into alien country, with Ben' (p. 89). What Harriet chooses is responsibility for Ben, a choice that does take her into an 'alien country' as more and more of her energy is directed toward controlling Ben so that he can fit in a family that does not have a place for him. Once again, Lessing dramatises the woman's role as care-taker.

Harriet's choice inevitably leads to a change deftly captured in her views of difference. Initially she smugly dismisses her sister's child born with Down's syndrome: 'of course she knew one shouldn't call them mongol. But the little girl did look a bit like Genghis Khan, didn't she?' (FC, p.22). Then in the 'place in the North of England', she sees its inmates as 'freaks' and 'monsters'. Only after accepting the task of rearing Ben does Harriet begin to look behind labels that contain the different; her proximity to Ben makes her begin to wonder 'what he wanted, what he felt' (FC, p. 116).

But Harriet's success, on one level, Ben's being removed from the institution, leads to failure with her 'real children'. One by one, Luke, Helen, Jane, and Paul (the most affected by his mother's choice), are taken and reared by members of the extended family. Once again, Lessing shows that choices have their costs. Harriet recognises that 'she had dealt the family a mortal wound when she rescued Ben' (F.C. p. 93), and even as Harriet's view is presented most sympathetically, the narrative does not shy away from questioning the choice and the cost. David's question – ' "And the four we have don't count?" ' (FC, p. 93) – haunts the narrative. Nor does Lessing disregard the guilt and self-pity that account for much of what Harriet does ('She wanted to be acknowledged, her predicament given its value' [FC, p. 103].). At the same time, Harriet's passion to understand is not ignored:

> Did he feel her eyes on him, as a human would? He sometimes looked at her while she looked at him – not often, but it did happen that his eyes met hers. She would put into her gaze these speculations, these queries, her need, her *passion* to know more about him – whom, after all, she had given birth to, had carried for eight months, though it nearly killed her – but he did not feel the questions she was asking. Indifferently, casually, he looked away again, and his eyes went to the faces of his mates, his followers.
>
> (FC, p. 131)

While never able fully to understand Ben, Harriet is able to 'socialise' him. In as trenchant a critique of society as she offers in any of her novels, Lessing shows Ben fitting in because society is breaking down. In the years after Ben's homecoming, the outside world has become a place of 'Wars and riots; killings and hijackings; murders and thefts and kidnappings . . . the eighties, the barbarous eighties were getting into their stride' (FC, p. 107). The society, itself, is becoming a throwback and Ben fits in, becoming the leader of a band of schoolmates, 'the uneducable, the unassimilable, the hopeless' (FC, p. 120) who temporarily occupy the rooms abandoned by the Lovatts' 'real children'. At the end of Lessing's family novel for the 1980s, Ben finds his acceptance in gang life and his calling in casual urban violence; Harriet and David prepare to sell the house to be free of Ben and his mates. In *The Fifth Child* Lessing produces a family novel about emotions *and* ideas, a novel that continues to demonstrate what Dee Seligman has called 'Doris Lessing's uncanny ability to touch the pulse of the present.'[12]

8 'The Battle of the Books': Lessing and the Critics

> What we need more than anything else, I am convinced, is some serious criticism. The most exciting periods of literature have always been those when the critics were great.
>
> Lessing (SPV, p. 14)

While never succumbing to Charlotte Brontë's direct overture to her 'Dear Reader', Doris Lessing has been canny in ways of trying to shape the reader's response to her fiction. I have drawn the epigraph for this chapter from 'The Small Personal Voice', first published in 1957. In that essay, Lessing's call for 'serious criticism' springs as much from her annoyance at reviews of *Martha Quest* and *A Proper Marriage* as it does from her overview of the contemporary British novel (deficient) in relation to nine-teenth-century fiction (great, particularly if written by the French or the Russians). Lessing's call chides what she saw as the effeteness of contemporary British criticism:

> As long as critics are as 'sensitive', subjective, and uncommitted to anything but their own private sensibilities, there will be no body of criticism worth taking seriously in this country. At the moment our critics remind me of a lot of Victorian ladies making out their library lists: this is a 'nice' book; or it is not a 'nice' book; the characters are 'nice'; or they are not 'nice'.
>
> (SPV, p. 14)

Latent in Lessing's comment is something of the anxiety that I discussed in Chapter 7; there the novel of ideas is implicitly gendered as male and the novel of emotions implicitly gendered as female or at least androgynous. In the preceding quotation, Lessing links 'private sensibilities' to Victorian ladies in a way that recalls George Eliot's distancing her seriousness from her silly female contemporaries. What Lessing seems to envision in 'The Small Personal Voice' is a robust criticism of ideas equal to what she sees herself doing in the robust novel of ideas represented by the first two volumes of *Children of Violence*.

Lessing's call for a 'serious criticism' in 'The Small Personal Voice' was the first important instance of what has become a cottage industry for her: admonishing critics (usually academic) and directing readers.[1] The admonitions and directions find their way into attachments, prefaces and afterwords, to many of her novels and interviews with critics (mostly academic). Eve Bertelsen has written a very important analysis of the dynamics of an interview with Doris Lessing which she describes as 'something like a battle'.[2] Using her own 1986 interview with Lessing as a base, Bertelsen explores Lessing's attempts to control the discourse. It seems to me that Bertelsen's comments are applicable to any number of interviews that Lessing has given over the years. What I want to consider here is another attempt at control, Lessing's use of attachments to her novels. The most striking example of that attempt is, of course, the celebrated 'Preface' to *The Golden Notebook* published nine years after the novel. In the 'Preface', Lessing stakes out her highly individualistic position as author/critic/teacher and proceeds to attack misreadings of the novel by reviewers and critics.

Although she uses the terms reviewer and critic interchangeably, Lessing seems most at war with the term critic.

About the critic and *The Golden Notebook*, Lessing writes:

> I thought that for the most part the criticism was too
> silly to be true. Recovering balance, I understood the
> problem. It is that writers are looking in the critics for an
> *alter ego*, that other self more intelligent than oneself
> who has seen what one is reaching for, and who judges
> you only by whether you have matched your aim or not.
> I have never met a writer who, faced at last with that
> rare being, a real critic, doesn't lose all paranoia and
> become gratefully attentive – he has found what he
> thinks he needs. But what he, the writer, is asking is
> impossible. Why should he expect this extraordinary
> being, the perfect critic (who does occasionally exist),
> why should there be anyone else who comprehends what
> he is trying to do? After all, there is only one person
> spinning that particular cocoon, only one person whose
> business it is to spin it.
>
> (GN, xv)

In some ways, the Lessing who seeks 'the perfect critic' is
like Anna Wulf who seeks to write the perfect novel.
Neither is satisfied with the ordinary or imperfect. Lessing
the author, however, shapes Anna the character's triumph
around an acceptance of the ordinary. Not so Lessing the
author's response to the critic.

Turning to the reason for the critic's failure to be 'real'
or 'perfect', Lessing berates the educational system from
which she had 'a lucky escape' at 14 (GN, xviii). The
system moulds students whose 'imaginative and original
judgement' is suppressed (GN, xvi). The university system
is the worst culprit, particularly the theses factories in the
United States. Having gone through such a mill, the critic
can do little more than 'patronise and itemise' (GN, xx). I
have abbreviated much of Lessing's critique of the educa-

tional system in the 'Preface', a critique present in a variety
of mutations from *Martha Quest* through *The Fifth Child*.
Many of her criticisms hit the mark, especially for those of
us involved in the work of education. But what I want to
suggest here is that some of the hectoring tone in Lessing's
critique of the academy is defensive. She is once more the
outsider trying to empower herself against insiders.

One effective way of doing this is to write against
academic canon-making: 'thirty or forty years ago, a critic
made a private list of writers and poets which he, person-
ally, considered made up what was valuable in literature,
dismissing all others' (GN, xix). At the same time, Lessing
is a canon-maker in her 'Preface' where she notes that 'the
book is more in the European tradition than the English
tradition of the novel. Or rather, in the English tradition as
viewed at the moment. The English novel after all does
include *Clarissa* and *Tristram Shandy*, *The Tragic Come-
dians* – and Joseph Conrad' (GN, xiv). Another of
Lessing's strategies is to enshrine autodidactism, her own
way of learning, as when she advises students: 'Those of
you who are more robust and individual than others, will
be encouraged to leave and find ways of educating yourself
– educating your own judgement' (GN, xvii).

Lessing's most interesting gambit, however, is to turn
herself into her own critic, whether 'real' or 'perfect', and
analyse *The Golden Notebook* for her ideal reader. She
explains what the book is not, principally 'not a trumpet
for Women's Liberation' (GN, ix). It is a novel of ideas
which comments on its own form as well as on 'the
intellectual and moral climate' of its time (GN, x). It is
also an exploration of the artist's attempt 'to deal with the
problem of "subjectivity", that shocking business of being
preoccupied with the tiny individual' (GN, xii). In the
'Preface' Lessing attempts to transform herself into 'that
other self more intelligent than oneself who has seen what

one is reaching for' and do away with the middle man, the unreal and imperfect critic.

Other more abridged attempts to direct the reader's view of the cocoon she has spun follow *The Golden Notebook*. Her 'Author's Notes' to *The Four-Gated City* offer her judgement that 'This book is what the Germans call a *Bildungsroman*' (F-G, 615), a judgement possibly calculated to offset criticism of the novel's non-traditional form. Then there is the 'Afterword, or End-Paper: A Small, Relevant Reminiscence' attached to *Briefing for a Descent into Hell*. That 'Afterword' reinscribes the novel's chief targets: the educational system and psychiatry. Less cryptic is the critical apparatus she constructs for *Canopus in Argos*.

First, Lessing offers 'Some Remarks' for *Shikasta*, wherein she creates a straw woman 'fed too long on the pieties of academia' (S, ix) as a way of telling the reader that it is all right to take space fiction seriously – very seriously. Lessing moves from showing how space fiction has 'set [me] free to be as experimental as I like, and as traditional' (S, ix). Actually, more traditional than experimental, as Lessing goes on to connect space fiction with science, sociology, and narratives like the Bible and the Koran: 'They have also explored the sacred literatures of the world in the same bold ways they take scientific and social possibilities to their logical conclusions so that we may examine them' (S, x). The reader has her cues for reading *Shikasta*, perhaps too many cues in light of the 'Preface' to *The Sirian Experiments*.

The reception of *Shikasta*, whether by critic or reader, compels Lessing to clarify what she is reaching for: 'if I have created a cosmology, then it is only for literary purposes' (SE, vii). She retreats from the more lavish claims of her remarks attached to *Shikasta* and finds some refuge in subjectivity. Once more, the issue of credentials: 'If I were a physicist there would be no trouble at all [in speculating]' (SE, vi); once more, the non-*auto da fé*: 'I do not "believe" that there are aliens on our moon – but why not' (SE, ix). Finally, a less ambitious aim for the series: 'I would so like it if reviewers and readers could see this series, *Canopus in Argos: Archives*, as a framework that enables me to tell (I hope) a beguiling tale or two; to put questions, both to myself and to others; to explore ideas and sociological possibilities' (SE, ix).

By the time she publishes *The Making of the Representative for Planet 8*, Lessing offers an 'Afterword' that 'should be considered as belonging to both *The Sirian Experiments* and *The Making of the Representative for Planet 8*, though more to the first than the second' (P8, p. 123). That strange qualification introduces about twenty pages of memoir/cultural criticism/ sociological rumination centring on Scott's expeditions to the Antarctic. Contrasting contemporary attitudes toward Scott's expedition with the accounts written by the explorers themselves, Lessing is more concerned with reading culture than with directing the reading of individual novels.

Her cultural criticism is a confusing mix at best which leads me to wonder why the 'Afterword' was published, a wonder centring on her comments about publishers:

There is a practical reason why it is a good thing the afterword is in the back of the short book, though it was not planned. When I told the English publisher this fourth volume would be very short, he was pleased, and not only because this would mean less trees, paper, printers' work, ink, bindings, but because in this country there is a bias in favour of short books, much more likely to be good ones, and of real quality, than long ones, and this in spite of Dickens and all those wordy and indubitably first-rate Victorians. Whereas, when I said to my American publisher that it was so short, he said at once, mocking himself and his nation, but meaning it, in the way they have over there, 'But you *know* that we can take only big books seriously.' So over there (or over here, according to how you look at it) big *is* beautiful after all.

(P8, pp.123–4)

I quote at length because Lessing's view is so intriguing. Throughout her career, Lessing has staged the battle between big and small novels in a variety of settings : in essays like 'The Small Personal Voice', in Anna Wulf's creative dilemma in *The Golden Notebook*, in her own pull between single novels and series. In those settings, the contest has had ideological ramifications (as in traditional *vs.* experimental or ideas *vs.* emotions). What interests me about the comments attached to *The Making of a Representative for Planet 8* is that the 'practical reason' (which, incidentally, Lessing never clarifies) seems to be a question of packaging, even of filler. Up to now, I have been tracking Lessing's involvement with critic/reviewer and reader. Now I would like to add publisher to the cast of characters, an addition that is as good a way as any to turn to *The Diaries of Jane Somers*.

Before being published as *The Diaries of Jane Somers* under Lessing's name, the two volumes that make up that volume, *The Diary of a Good Neighbour* and *If the Old Could . . .* were published under Jane Somers's name. Jane Somers's first novel was published as Doris Lessing was completing *Canopus in Argos*, and as Lessing makes clear in her 'Preface' to *The Diaries of Jane Somers*, the novels are related. Lessing offers three reasons for writing under a pseudonym, the third of which relates to *Canopus in Argos*. First, she writes of wanting to be reviewed as a new writer, an aim which Ellen Goodman calls 'an extraordinary, vulnerable piece of personal risk-taking, this proud hoax'.[3] That first reason is linked to her second aim: 'I

wanted to cheer up young writers, who often have such a
hard time of it' (DJS, vii). Established writers, too, can
experience hard times, and it is Lessing's third reason that
most interests me. 'Another reason, frankly if faintly
malicious: some reviewers complained they hated my
Canopus series, why didn't I write realistically, the way I
used to do before: preferably *The Golden Notebook* over
again? These were sent *The Diary of a Good Neighbour* but
not one recognised me' (DJS, vii). Once again, 'the perfect
critic' is missing. Or perhaps I should write, twice again: in
rejecting *Canopus in Argos* and in not recognising *The
Diary of a Good Neighbour*.

Given Lessing's fairly consistent criticism of critics, the
remarks in the 'Preface' are almost predictable; Lessing
wants 'to get free of that cage of associations and labels'
(DJS, vii). But critics are not the only readers deceived by
Jane Somers (aka Doris Lessing). *The Diary of a Good
Neighbour* was turned down by Lessing's British publishers, Jonathan Cape and Granada. According to Lessing,
the manuscript was rejected because:

> it was too depressing to publish: in these fallen days
> major and prestigious publishers can see nothing wrong
> in refusing a novel in which they see merit because it
> might not sell. Not thus, once, were serious literary
> publishers.
>
> (DJS, ix)

The word 'serious' surfaces later in the 'Preface' when she
makes a distinction between writers in order to make a
point about publishers:

> One of the problems of the 'serious' as distinct from the
> 'commercial' author is this attitude on the part of his or
> her publisher. You are pressured to do interviews,

television, and so on, but you are conscious that the more you agree, the more you are earning his or her contempt.

(DJS, xi)

Lessing's remarks in the 'Preface' are not the first time she has voiced her disquiet with the commercial aspects of publishing, sequences in *The Golden Notebook* and the 'Author's Notes' to *The Four-Gated City* come immediately to mind. Nonetheless the comments attached to *The Diaries of Jane Somers* are Lessing's most involved and self-interested presentation of the relationship among writer, publisher, reviewer, and reader. In Lessing's presentation of her 'little experiment' (DJS, vii) writers, whether new or established, are victims of commerce: many have become part of the sales departments of their publishers' (DJS, xi). Writers are also the prey of 'most reviewers and readers [who] want you to go on writing the same book' (DJS, xi). In the relationship among writer, publisher, reviewer, and reader, then, Lessing can easily identify three culprits in 'that whole dreadful process in book publishing that "nothing succeeds like success" '.[4]

Jonathan Yardley comments on a significant omission in Lessing's exposé of 'that whole dreadful process':

Certainly a success syndrome exists in the book industry, and reviewers are susceptible to it as well as publishers. But it also exists in the minds of writers, an aspect of the situation that is conveniently ignored in Lessing's argument. If it is true that famous authors too often get free rides from publishers and critics, then it is equally true that famous authors *expect* free rides. The ego of the author can be a monumental thing – especially, need it be said, that of a famous one – and it can lead the author to believe that everything he or she writes is a work of genius. This as it happens, is not always true, but one constant remains: Famous authors expect all their books to be published, to be praised, and to sell.[5]

Yardley's commentary brings me back to my interest in Lessing's 'frankly if faintly malicious' third reason for her 'little experiment', some reviewers' negative responses to *Canopus in Argos*. Here I want to half-agree with Ellen Goodman who notes 'Doris Lessing is too world-wise to be victimised by vanity.'[6] Lessing is world-wise and nobody's victim. She is, in fact, 'world-wise' enough to create her 'little experiment' as a way of getting maximum attention for her attack on what she sees as misreadings by publishers, reviewers, and readers alike – experiences common to Jane Somers and Doris Lessing.

Jane Somers, though, never suffers directly at the hands of academic critics as Doris Lessing has. Yet lurking behind some of the labelling that Lessing lambasts and the attitudes toward 'the "serious" as distinct from the "commercial" author' that affect publishers' decisions are academics, a favoured target for Lessing. Throughout her career, Lessing has been highly, and often accurately, critical of the educational system. As she notes:

> It starts when the child is as young as five or six, when he arrives at school. It starts with marks, rewards, 'places', 'streams', stars – and still in many places, stripes. This horse-race mentality, the victor and loser way of thinking, leads to 'Writer X is, is not, a few paces ahead of Writer Y. Writer Y has fallen behind. In his last book Writer Z has shown himself as better than Writer A.' From the beginning the child is trained to think in this way: always in terms of comparison, of success, and of failure.
>
> (GN, xv)

Nowhere is the 'horse-race mentality' more apparent, according to Lessing, than in the university, 'an international system, absolutely identical from the Urals to Yugoslavia, from Minnesota to Manchester' (GN, xvii).

Two interviews with Lessing in 1984 capture her long-lived antipathy to academic institutions. In a discussion with Eve Bertelsen, Lessing, once again, criticises the critics:

As you know they're not very bright. I hate to say this, but I've been steadily appalled at the level of criticism. There are more and more critics all the time, everywhere. Simply because there're more and more people, and more and more universities – it's an industry. But the standards get lower and lower. There are very few critics that I'm interested in. You know the university scene. It isn't a help to literature, it's the opposite.[7]

In April of that same year when talking to Susan Stamberg, Lessing describes standardised university thinking: 'I was up in a university last week and it was almost funny. Every question, until I punched it up, without exception was, "Mrs Lessing, is it this or is it that; do you do this or that?" '[8]

Despite Lessing's frequent dismissal of academics, her status as a 'serious' rather than 'commercial' writer has a good deal to do with her reception by the academic world. She is, after all, one living writer with both a scholarly society, the Doris Lessing Society, and a publication, *The Doris Lessing Newsletter*, named for her. The society owes much to the pioneering work of Paul Schlueter who chaired the first panel on Lessing at the 1971 meeting of the Modern Language Association, a primary academic organisation in the United States. The newsletter, first published in 1976, is the work of Dee Seligman.

Academic interest in Lessing came at a time when younger members of the profession, many of them women, were as critical of the university system and its hierarchies as Lessing herself has been. Lessing had a following, even a fan club. She was the perfect maverick writer who could not be easily categorised for a generation of academics who were hostile to and critical of academic categories. The rebel with many causes, Lessing, the outsider, had made it inside. Yet true to her own integrity and her pride in and anxiety about her 'lucky escape' from formal education, Lessing criticises even her own special status in the academy. Responding to a question in an interview with Eve Bertelsen, Lessing talks of her acute embarrassment with *The Doris Lessing Newsletter*: 'I don't like the cult atmosphere at all.'[9] The insider is outside once again – but not quite.

As a result of academic interest, Lessing's novels are now frequently assigned reading in college and university courses in the United States. And having so often faced the difficulty of finding reasonably priced editions of Lessing's novels for graduate and undergraduate courses that I have taught, I appreciate the argument made by Ellen Cronan Rose. After noting that in the late 1980s only *The Golden Notebook* is available 'in a mass-market' paperback and that other Lessing novels are available only in pricey Plume and Vintage editions, Rose observes:

Undeniably these facts reflect recent mergers and acquisitions in the publishing industry. But they also probably reflect market research that tells publishers what audience to target for a particular book or author. Publishers have apparently concluded that Lessing's appeal, now, is primarily to academics. Plume and Vintage paperbacks are not only more expensive than the Bantam, Ballantine and Popular Library paperbacks in which Lessing was packaged in the seventies; they also have wide

margins (convenient for note-taking) and are distribu-
ted not in supermarkets but in bookshops, principally
though not exclusively in university bookshops.[10]

For good or ill, Lessing's reputation as a 'serious' writer, a
standing that she has sought from the beginning of her
career, largely derives from readers 'fed too long on the
pieties of academia'.

Notes

Notes to Chapter 1

1. C. J. Driver, 'Profile 8: Doris Lessing', *The New Review*, 18 (Nov. 1974), p. 21.

2. Lessing's Foreword to Lawrence Vambe's *An Ill-Fated People: Zimbabwe Before and After Rhodes* reprinted as 'Lessing on Zimbabwe', *Doris Lessing Newsletter*, 4, 1 (Summer 1980), p. 11.

3. 'Lessing on Zimbabwe', p. 12.

4. Doris Lessing, 'Impertinent Daughters', *Granta*, 14 (1984), p. 54.

5. Nicole Ward Jouve, 'Of mud and other matter – *The Children of Violence*', *Notebooks/Memoirs/ Archives: Reading and Rereading Doris Lessing*, ed. Jenny Taylor (London: Routledge & Kegan Paul, 1982), p. 104.

6. Jouve, 'Of mud and other matter – *The Children of Violence*', p. 104.

7. Claire Sprague, '*The Golden Notebook*: In Whose or What Great Tradition? *Approaches to Teaching Lessing's 'The Golden Notebook'*, ed., Carey Kaplan and Ellen Cronan Rose (New York: The Modern Language Association of America, 1989), p. 78.

8. Walter Allen, *Tradition and Dream: The English and American Novel From the Twenties to Our Time* (London: Phoenix House, 1964), p. 276.

9. Deirdre David, *Intellectual Women and Victorian Patriarchy* (Ithaca: Cornell University Press, 1987), p. 163.

10. Sprague, '*The Golden Notebook*: In Whose or What Great Tradition', p. 82.

11. Tom Maschler, *Declaration* (London: MacGibbon & Kee, 1957), p. 12.

12. Lorna Sage, *Doris Lessing* (London: Methuen, 1983), p. 11.

Notes to Chapter 2

1. Olive Schreiner, *The Story of an African Farm* (Chicago: Donohue, Henneberry & Co, 1883), p. 228.

2. Sage, *Doris Lessing*, pp. 27–8.

3. Ruth Whittaker, *Doris Lessing* (New York: St Martin's Press, 1988), p. 27.

4. Whittaker, *Doris Lessing*, p. 28.

5. The original title is recorded by Eve Bertelsen, 'The Quest and the Quotidian: Doris Lessing in South Africa', *In Pursuit of Doris Lessing: Nine Nations Reading*, ed. Claire Sprague (New York: St Martin's Press, 1990), p. 44.

6. Lessing's overriding interest in white Africans in her novels and short stories is one element in her marginalisation by Zimbabwean readers, a situation analysed by Anthony Chennells in 'Reading Doris Lessing's Rhodesian Stories in Zimbabwe', *In Pursuit of Doris Lessing*, pp. 17–40.

7. Olive Schreiner, too, exploited the power of dreams, especially as a key to mystical experience. She published a book called *Dreams* in 1891.

8. Schreiner, *The Story of an African Farm*, p. 200.

9. George Levine, *The Realistic Imagination: English Fiction from Frankenstein to Lady Chatterley* (Chicago: University of Chicago Press, 1981), p. 56.

10. Schreiner, *The Story of an African Farm*, p. 8.

11. George Levine has convincingly argued for realism's ability to accommodate such expansion: *The Realistic Imagination*, p. 56.

12. Nancy Bazin, 'The Moment of Revelation in *Martha Quest* and Comparable Moments by Two Modernists', *Modern Fiction Studies*, Doris Lessing Number, vol. 26, no. 1 (Spring 1980), p. 87.

13. Bazin, 'The Moment of Revelation', p. 95.

Notes to Chapter 3

1. Susan Brownmiller, ' "Best Battles Are Fought by Men and Women Together" ', *Critical Essays on Doris Lessing*, eds Claire Sprague and Virginia Tiger (Boston: G.K. Hall, 1986), p. 220.

2. Virginia Tiger, 'Candid Shot: Lessing in New York City, April 1 and 2, 1984', *Critical Essays on Doris Lessing*, p. 221.

3. In ' "Best Battles Are Fought by Men and Women Together" ', Susan Brownmiller quotes Lessing as saying 'I don't believe in getting married, unless you have children. I don't like marriage at all. I've had two of them', p. 220.

4. In 'Of mud and other matter – *The Children of Violence*', Nicole Ward Jouve notes: 'The first four volumes of *The Children of Violence*, though they are preoccupied with racial issues, though the existence of the many white characters who appear is based on the *labour* of the black Africans, ignore that labour', p. 99.

5. In '*Veldtanschauung*: Doris Lessing's Savage Africa', Eve Bertelsen explores this issue using *The Grass Is Singing* as central text. *Modern Fiction Studies*, vol. 37, no. 4 (Winter 1991), pp. 647–58.

6. Jenny Taylor, 'Introduction: Situating Reading', *Notebooks/Memoirs/Archives*, p. 6.

7. Margaret Drabble, 'Doris Lessing: Cassandra in a World under Siege', *Critical Essays on Doris Lessing*, p. 188.

8. Jean McCrindle, 'Reading *The Golden Notebook* in 1962', *Notebooks/Memoirs/Archives*, p. 44.

9. Elizabeth Wilson, 'Yesterday's Heroines: On Rereading Lessing and de Beauvoir', *Notebooks/Memoirs/Archives*, p. 57.

10. Lee T. Lemon, *Portraits of the Artist in Contemporary Fiction* (Lincoln: University of Nebraska, 1985), p. 59.

11. Levine, *The Realistic Imagination*, p. 6.

12. N. Katherine Hayles, *Chaos Bound: Orderly Disorder in Contemporary Literature and Science* (Ithaca: Cornell University Press), 1990, p. 265.

13. Hayles, *Chaos Bound*, pp. 246–7.

14. Taylor, 'Introduction: Situating Reading', p. 9.

15. Rachel Brownstein, *Becoming a Heroine: Reading About Women in Novels* (New York: Viking Press, 1982), p. 26.

16. Virginia Woolf, 'Professions for Women', *Women and Writing*, ed. Michele Barrett (New York: Harcourt Brace Jovanovich, 1979), pp. 61–2.

17. Margaret Moan Rowe, 'Muriel Spark and the Angel of the Body', *Critique* (Spring 1987), pp. 167–76.

18. Many readers of Lessing's work have made comparisons between sexual maps drawn by Lawrence and Lessing. One of the most interesting comparisons is Mark Spilka's in 'Lessing and Lawrence: The Battle of the Sexes', *Critical Essays on Doris Lessing*, pp. 69–86.

Notes to Chapter 4

1. Sage, *Doris Lessing*, p. 59.

2. Roberta Rubenstein marks this doubleness when she notes: 'The novel unfolds on two levels simultaneously: the literal and the phenomenal plane traces the development of events in the macrocosm, the world of other people, while the symbolic plane connects those events to the microcosm of Martha's own consciousness.' *The Novelistic Vision of Doris Lessing: Breaking the Forms of Consciousness* (Urbana: University of Illinois Press, 1979), p. 130.

3. Jeannette King, *Doris Lessing* (London: Edward Arnold, 1989), p. 26.

4. Gore Vidal, 'Paradise Regained', *Critical Essays on Doris Lessing*, p. 200.

5. Gillian Beer, *Darwin's Plots: Evolutionary Narrative in Darwin, George Eliot and Nineteenth-Century Fiction* (London: Ark Paperbacks, 1985), p. 175.

6. Gordon S. Haight, *George Eliot: A Biography* (Oxford: Clarendon Press, 1968), p. 36.

7. George Eliot, 'Silly Novels by Lady Novelists', *Essays of George Eliot*, ed. Thomas Pinney (London: Routledge & Kegan Paul, 1963), p. 310.

8. Eliot, *Essays*, p. 314.

9. Gillian Beer, *Darwin's Plots*, p. 181.

10. Gillian Beer, *Darwin's Plots*, p. 184.

Notes to Chapter 5

1. R. D. Laing, 'Preface to the Pelican Edition', *The Divided Self* (New York: Penguin Books, 1965), p. 11.

2. 'The Sufi Path' quoted by Idries Shah, *The Way of the Sufi* (New York: Penguin Books, 1974), p. 295.

3. Joan Didion, 'Review of *Briefing for a Descent Into Hell*', *Critical Essays on Doris Lessing*, p. 194.

4. Lawrence, *Letters*, vol. II, ed. George Zytaruk and James Boulton (Cambridge: Cambridge University Press, 1981), p. 183.

5. Rubenstein, *The Novelistic Vision of Doris Lessing*, p. 178.

6. Katherine Fishburn, *The Unexpected Universe of Doris Lessing: A Study in Narrative Technique* (Westport, Connecticut: Greenwood Press, 1985), p. 34.

7. Fishburn, *The Unexpected Universe*, p. 34.

8. Betsy Draine, *Substance Under Pressure: Artistic Coherence and Evolving Form in the Novels of Doris Lessing* (Madison: The University of Wisconsin Press, 1983), p. 105.

9. Sage, *Doris Lessing*, p. 68.

10. Whittaker, *Doris Lessing*, p. 90.

11. Fishburn, *The Unexpected Universe*, p. 13.

12. Sage, *Doris Lessing*, p. 76.

Notes to Chapter 6

1. W. B. Yeats, 'Under Ben Bulben', *Collected Poems* (New York: Macmillan, 1956), p. 344.

2. Sage, *Doris Lessing*, p. 77.

3. Jouve, 'Of mud and other matter – *The Children of Violence*', pp. 124–5.

4. Whittaker, *Doris Lessing*, p. 99.

5. Claire Sprague, *Rereading Doris Lessing: Narrative Patterns of Doubling and Repetition* (Chapel Hill: University of North Carolina Press, 1987), p. 174.

6. *The Radical Imagination and the Liberal Tradition: Interviews with English and American Novelists*, ed. Heide Ziegler and Christopher Bigsby (London: Junction Books, 1982), p. 203.

7. I am aware that Lessing moves agilely away from the question of what she herself believes about the world she has created in *Canopus in Argos*. See, for example, her 'Preface' to *The Sirian Experiments*.

8. Sage, *Doris Lessing*, p. 82.

9. Shikasta (the hurt) was originally called Rohanda (the fruitful).

10. Draine, *Substance Under Pressure*, p. 174.

11. Fishburn, *The Unexpected Universe*, p. 99.

12. Marsha Rowe, ' "If you mate a swan and a gander, who will ride?" ', *Notebooks/Memoirs/Archives*, p. 197.

13. Draine, *Substance Under Pressure*, p. 164.

14. King, *Doris Lessing*, p. 82.

15. Sprague, *Rereading Doris Lessing*, p. 132.

16. Sprague, *Rereading Doris Lessing*, p. 121.

17. Draine, *Substance Under Pressure*, p. 176

18. Fishburn, *The Unexpected Universe*, p. 133.

Notes to Chapter 7

1. Robert Frost, 'Desert Places', *The Poetry of Robert Frost*, ed. Edward Connery Lathem (New York: Holt, Rinehart & Winston, 1975), p. 296.

2. Bigsby, *The Radical Imagination and the Liberal Tradition*, pp. 204–5.

3. Judith Kegan Gardiner, *Rhys, Stead, Lessing, and the Politics of Empathy* (Bloomington: Indiana University Press, 1989), p. 119.

4. Sprague, *Rereading Doris Lessing*, p. 120.

5. Whittaker, *Doris Lessing*, p. 122.

6. Whittaker, *Doris Lessing*, p. 129.

7. Draine, *Substance Under Pressure*, p. 167.

8. Joseph Conrad, *The Secret Agent* (New York: Doubleday Anchor Books, 1953), p.11.

9. Sprague, *Rereading Doris Lessing*, p. 112.

10. Hans-Peter Rodenberg, '*The Fifth Child*: An Interview with Doris Lessing', *Doris Lessing Newsletter*, vol. 13, no. 1 (Summer 1989), p. 3.

11. Rodenberg, '*The Fifth Child*: An Interview With Doris Lessing', p. 3.

12. Dee Seligman, 'In Pursuit of Doris Lessing', *Approaches to Teaching Lessing's Golden Notebook*, p. 21.

Notes to Chapter 8

1. John Leonard offers a more negative view of Lessing's aim which in 'The Spacing Out of Doris Lessing', he describes as her attempt 'to bully the reader', *Critical Essays on Doris Lessing*, p. 205.

2. Eve Bertelsen, 'Who is it who says "I"?: The Persona of a Doris Lessing Interview', *Doris Lessing: The Alchemy of Survival*, ed. Carey Kaplan and Ellen Cronan Rose (Athens: Ohio University Press, 1988), p. 173.

3. Ellen Goodman, 'The Doris Lessing Hoax', *Critical Essays on Doris Lessing*, p. 214.

4. Goodman, 'The Doris Lessing Hoax', p. 213.

5. Jonathan Yardley, 'Lessing Is More: An "Unknown" Author and the Success Syndrome', *Critical Essays on Doris Lessing*, p. 215.

6. Goodman, 'The Doris Lessing Hoax', p. 214.

7. Eve Bertelsen, 'Interview with Doris Lessing (London, 9 January 1984)', *Doris Lessing*, ed. Eve Bertelsen (Johannesburg: McGraw-Hill, 1985), p. 97.

8. Susan Stamberg, 'An Interview with Doris Lessing', *Doris Lessing Newsletter*, vol. 8, no. 2 (Fall 1984) p. 4.

9. Bertelsen, 'Interview with Doris Lessing (London, 9 January 1984)', p. 93.

10. Ellen Cronan Rose, 'From Supermarket to Schoolroom', *In Pursuit of Doris Lessing*, p. 81.

Select Bibliography

Allen, Walter, *Tradition and Dream: The English and American Novel From the Twenties to Our Time* (London: Phoenix House, 1964).

Bazin, Nancy, 'The Moment of Revelation in *Martha Quest* and Comparable Moments by Two Modernists', *Modern Fiction Studies* 26, no. 1 (Spring 1980), pp. 87–98.

Beer, Gillian, *Darwin's Plots: Evolutionary Narrative in Darwin, George Eliot and Nineteenth-Century Fiction* (London: Ark Paperbacks, 1985).

Bertelsen, Eve (ed.), *Doris Lessing* (Johannesburg: McGraw-Hill, 1985).

Bertelsen, Eve, 'Veldtanschauung: Doris Lessing's Savage Africa', *Modern Fiction Studies*, 37, no. 4 (Winter 1991), pp. 647–58.

Brownstein, Rachel, *Becoming a Heroine: Reading About Women in Novels* (New York: The Viking Press, 1982).

Conrad, Joseph, *The Secret Agent* (New York: Doubleday Anchor Books, 1953).

David, Deirdre, *Intellectual Women and Victorian Patriarchy* (Ithaca: Cornell University Press, 1987).

Draine, Betsy, *Substance Under Pressure: Artistic Coherence and Evolving Form in the Novels of Doris Lessing* (Madison: The University of Wisconsin Press, 1983).

Driver, C. J., 'Profile 8: Doris Lessing', *The New Review*, 18 (Nov. 1974), pp. 17–23.

Eliot, George, *Essays*, ed. Thomas Pinney (London: Routledge & Kegan Paul, 1963).

Fishburn, Katherine, *The Unexpected Universe of Doris Lessing: A Study in Narrative Technique* (Westport, Connecticut: Greenwood Press, 1985).

Frost, Robert, *The Poetry of Robert Frost*, ed. Edward Connery Lathem (New York: Holt, Rinehart & Winston, 1975).

Gardiner, Judith Kegan, *Rhys, Stead, Lessing, and the Politics of Empathy* (Bloomington: Indiana University Press, 1989).

Haight, Gordon S., *George Eliot: A Biography* (Oxford: Clarendon Press, 1968).

Hayles, N. Katherine, *Chaos Bound: Orderly Disorder in Contemporary Literature and Science* (Ithaca: Cornell University Press, 1990).

Kaplan, Carey and Rose, Ellen Cronan (eds), *Approaches to Teaching Lessing's 'The Golden Notebook'* (New York: The Modern Language Association of America, 1989).

King, Jeannette, *Doris Lessing* (London: Edward Arnold, 1989).

Laing, R. D., *The Divided Self* (New York: Penguin Books, 1965).

Lawrence, D. H., *Letters*, vol. II, ed. George Zytaruk and James Boulton (Cambridge: Cambridge University Press, 1981).

Lemon, Lee, *Portraits of the Artist in Contemporary Fiction* (Lincoln: University of Nebraska, 1985).

Lessing, Doris, 'Impertinent Daughters', *Granta*, 14 (1984), pp. 52–68.

Lessing, Doris, 'Lessing on Zimbabwe', *Doris Lessing Newsletter*, 4, no. 1 (Summer 1980), pp. 1 and 11–13.

Levine, George, *The Realistic Imagination: English Fiction from Frankenstein to Lady Chatterley* (Chicago: The University of Chicago Press, 1981).

Maschler, Tom, *Declaration* (London: MacGibbon & Kee, 1957).

Rodenberg, Hans-Peter, '*The Fifth Child*: An Interview with Doris Lessing', *Doris Lessing Newsletter*, 13, no. 1 (Summer 1989), pp. 3–4.

Rowe, Margaret Moan, 'Muriel Spark and the Angel of the Body', *Critique*, XXVIII (Spring 1987), pp. 167–76.

Rubenstein, Roberta, *The Novelistic Vision of Doris Lessing: Breaking the Forms of Consciousness* (Urbana: University of Illinois Press, 1979).

Sage, Lorna, *Doris Lessing* (London: Methuen, 1983).

Schreiner, Olive, *The Story of an African Farm* (Chicago: Donohue, Henneberry & Co., 1883).

Shah, Idries, *The Way of the Sufi* (New York: Penguin Books, 1974).

Sprague, Claire, *Rereading Doris Lessing: Narrative Patterns of Doubling and Repetition* (Chapel Hill: The University of North Carolina Press, 1987).

Sprague, Claire (ed.), *In Pursuit of Doris Lessing: Nine Nations Reading* (New York: St Martin's Press, 1990).

Sprague, Claire and Tiger, Virginia (eds), *Critical Essays on Doris Lessing* (Boston: G. K. Hall, 1986).

Stamberg, Susan, 'An Interview with Doris Lessing', *Doris Lessing Newsletter*, 8, no. 2 (Fall 1984), pp. 3–4 and 15.

Taylor, Jenny (ed.), *Notebooks/Memoirs/ Archives: Reading and Rereading Doris Lessing* (London: Routledge & Kegan Paul, 1982).

Whittaker, Ruth, *Doris Lessing* (New York: St Martin's Press, 1988).

Woolf, Virginia, *Women and Writing*, ed. Michele Barrett (New York: Harcourt Brace Jovanovich, 1979).

Yeats, W. B., *Collected Poems* (New York: Macmillan, 1956).

Ziegler, Heide and Bigsby, Christopher (eds), *The Radical Imagination and the Liberal Tradition: Interviews with English and American Novelists* (London: Junction Books, 1982).

Index